Girls' Own Stories

Jocelyn Robson and Beverley Zalcock

Girls' Own Stories
Australian and New Zealand Women's Films

Scarlet Press

Published by Scarlet Press
5 Montague Road, London E8 2HN

Copyright © Jocelyn Robson and Beverley Zalcock 1997

The authors assert their moral right to be identified as the authors of the work in accordance with the Copyright,
Design and Patents Act 1988

British Library Cataloguing-in-Publication Data
A catalogue record for this book is available from
the British Library
ISBN 1 85727 053 3 pb

All rights reserved. No part of this publication may be
reproduced or transmitted in any form or by any means,
electronic or mechanical, including photocopying, recording, or any
information storage and retrieval system, without permission in writing
from the publisher.

Designed and produced for Scarlet Press by
Chase Production Services, Chadlington, Oxford, OX7 3LN
Typeset from the author's disk by
Stanford DTP Services, Milton Keynes
Printed in Great Britain

Dedicated to our Mothers

Contents

Acknowledgements   viii

1. The Back Drop   1
2. Brilliant Beginnings   9
3. A New Zealand Landmark   19
4. Short Circuits   30
5. Other Identities   46
6. Child's-eye View   60
7. Celluloid Sisters   73
8. Disrupting the Family   86
9. Women Displaced   97
10. The Wave Rolls On   109

Notes   127
Select Bibliography   132
Filmography   135
Index   139

Acknowledgements

We have been helped by many people in many different places. In particular, we wish to thank the following:

Charlotte Baggins (London), Ann Beaton & Jenny Hudson (Australian Film Commission, London), Carol Biggs (London), Sarah Buist (London), Gregory Burke (Creative New Zealand, Wellington) Cairo Cannon (London), Sara Chambers (London), Kate Collier (Sydney), Helen de Witt (Cinenova, London), Catherine Fitzgerald & Phil Langridge (The New Zealand Film Commission, Wellington), Jan Hope (Auckland), Keely Macarow (London), Carol Morley (London), Margot Nash (Sydney), Diane Pivac & Bronwen Taylor (The New Zealand Film Archive, Wellington), and Katharine Robson (Wellington).

1

The Back Drop

'There's something Australasian going on among women's films,' remarked the respected New Zealand director Gaylene Preston in a recent interview: 'I think that women's work is not only having an effect at the box office . . . but also having an effect on what men might contemplate doing . . . And I get a funny feeling now that when we walk into the pub not all the backs are turned.'[1]

This book is our attempt to come to terms with that 'Australasian something', to explore its meanings and its distinctiveness, in the context of the last two decades and, particularly, in the wake of the women's movement of the 1970s. Until now, feminist debate has centred mainly on Hollywood cinema and it is clearly time to link some of these concerns to films emerging from other countries, where some quite specific preoccupations are evident.

The Funding Context
Before we begin, however, we need to set the scene. The question we want to ask here is: Why now? Why, that is, have these films been made at this time, in these countries? Part of the answer may lie in some specific features of both the industrial and the cultural context of the last two decades and while these are not, of course, identical for both countries (since each has its own specific nuances, its own history), there are, all the same, a number of similarities.

During the late 1970s and for part of the 1980s, there were tax concessions available in both Australia and New Zealand which were designed to encourage private investment in the film industry. These concessions followed a resurgence of film-making in the 1970s which both governments had sponsored and wanted to see maintained. The concessions ended in New Zealand in 1984, after a two-year extension to allow existing projects to be completed; they lasted slightly longer in Australia but were steadily reduced in the early 1980s and eventually brought to an end in 1988. The tax shelters did effectively stimulate production in both countries but, in many cases, it was the production of purely commercial films, with little or no indigenous character and increasing amounts of overseas participation. The systems were open to abuse and were blamed for undermining standards in the industry by offering investors the best returns on films that lost money.

Nevertheless, interest had been revived and valuable experience gained. Television was developing apace in both countries, and both were now committed to supporting industries that would never be self-sufficient in financial terms, but which might offer opportunities for representing and expressing their emerging and increasingly confident national identities. When the tax havens ended, government support was maintained in Australia chiefly through the setting up of the Film Finance Corporation, a new film investment body, in 1988. The role of the existing Australian Film Commission (AFC) was changed to give it more emphasis as a development agency for film production, alongside its cultural and research responsibilities. In New Zealand, government support was maintained through the New Zealand Film Commission (NZFC) which had been established in 1978. In both countries, the film commissions have had a commercial focus as well as an interest in supporting local projects which may serve to affirm and reflect the national culture. In the case of the NZFC, for example, the criteria for 'certification' as a 'New Zealand' film are explicitly stated in legislation and include consideration of subject and location, as well as the nationalities of director, actors and crew members. These requirements have without doubt influenced the kinds of projects which film-makers have embarked upon, especially in New Zealand and particularly in the last decade, and they certainly help to account for the character of the films which eventually find their way on to the screen.

Also important in the New Zealand context, in recent years, have been the Short Film Fund (which was set up as a division of the NZFC in 1985) and the Creative Film and Video Fund (which is supported by the arts council – renamed Creative New Zealand in 1995 – as well as by the NZFC and Television New Zealand). These funds have provided women (such as Alison Maclean and others) with the opportunity to gain experience as directors of short, often experimental, films which, as we have mentioned, often facilitates their move into mainstream feature film production. In Australia, even more significant perhaps has been the Women's Film Fund (WFF) which was set up in the mid-1970s, coinciding with both the revival of the Australian film industry and 1970s feminism. This fund was administered by the Australian Film Commission, and watched over by various interest groups (such as the Sydney Women's Film Group). The WFF (which was phased out in 1988) supported the production of many short films, particularly in the early 1980s, and it was actively involved in the distribution and exhibition of women's films, as well as in research and the training and employment of women in the industry.[2] The AFC now has a Women's Programme that funds workshops and training for potential women directors and it is worth noting that although there is now no specific affirmative funding policy in Australia, women in fact received around 50 per cent of the official funding available in 1995. The situation is currently less promising in New Zealand, unfortunately, where, by early 1996, the NZFC was reported to be in serious financial difficulty.

The general point, however, is that, when it is available, government money rarely brings with it the same commercial imperatives as private finance and the flexibility of the funding arrangements in both New Zealand and Australia, with their cultural as well as their commercial considerations, has given local directors a degree of freedom that the money-orientated studio-type system of Hollywood, for example, would be unlikely to accept. Although a small number of privately financed films continue to be made in both countries (*The Piano*, made in 1993, is a notable example), the fact that both industries continue to require government assistance in some form or other remains significant.

A similar pattern has emerged in Canada where, until the 1960s, virtually no feature films were made at all and the commercial industry was heavily dominated by US production. Then in 1968, the government started to sponsor films that would put on to the screens the people and concerns of Canada. Most of these projects had modest budgets and were never intended to rival or imitate the Hollywood blockbusters. In 1975, the National Film Board of Canada, in direct response to women's demands, founded Studio D, a section dedicated to making films by and about Canadian women. Slowly, but in increasing numbers, Canadian women have entered the feature film industry and films such as *My American Cousin* (Sandy Wilson, 1985) and the delightful *I've Heard the Mermaids Singing* (Patricia Rozema, 1987), which both received public funding, testify to their presence and their talent. Nevertheless, by 1990 women film-makers in Canada still accounted for only 3 per cent of the budget.[3]

By this time, mobility for women in Hollywood was increasing and a few women directors had broken in, usually with one-off projects, but in relation to the workforce as a whole women are still very much in a minority in the top jobs.[4] Further, the women who are directing in Hollywood (unlike most of their Australian, New Zealand and Canadian counterparts) are generally not making women-orientated films. In the publicly supported industries, women directors have had greater access and much more freedom, and, as Annette Kuhn notes in relation to the Canadian industry,[5] the women's movement has provided not only the will for women to enter the profession but often its subjects and sensibilities as well.

Cultural Considerations

Aspects of the cultural context in both Australia and New Zealand are also highly relevant to a discussion of their cinema, as are the various cultural identities (and perceptions of identity) that have underpinned life in these two colonies. We do not wish to imply that the cultures are homogeneous, monolithic or identical, but some simplification and generalisation about themes and emphases, about cultural dispositions, historical as well as current, may help to contextualise the films.

That both *were* colonies is highly significant. Writing about the Australian colonists, most of whom had penal origins and therefore had a tendency to see themselves as reluctant members of a dispossessed and despised society, Neil Rattigan says:

> Australians developed a culture based upon the rejection of much of the dominant colonising culture of England. Thus, while there was continuity of many of the ideological state apparatuses of England – legal system, Westminster system of government, public administration, education, church and so forth – a cultural identity developed which would become in turn a *national* identity based upon denial (as much as possible) of class distinction, based upon ideals of egalitarianism, collectivism, and the distinctly Australian mythos of mateship.[6]

There are resonances here that many New Zealanders will also recognise. The New Zealand settlers were not from penal backgrounds, were presumably therefore less 'reluctant' and may have felt less rejected by the parent culture. Arguably, there has been more emphasis in New Zealand on individualism and less on 'mateship' but the isolation and the enormous physical demands of the new environment and the need for survival here, too, did encourage collectivity to a certain extent, as well as the rejection of old priorities determined according to social status and a new emphasis on giving and getting a 'fair go'.

The experience of colonisation in both countries has helped to shape various images or myths of national identity. From the pioneer, the bushman, and the returning soldier, for example, came the more contemporary 'ocker' (Australia) or the 'Good Keen Man' (New Zealand), where the emphasis fell on unsophistication, on a celebration of vulgarity, on practicality, on 'doing it yourself', on a lack of deference and on anti-authoritarianism. The striking feature of all these identities is, of course, their maleness and their whiteness. Juliet Batten, a New Zealand artist, wrote in 1989:

> Why can't I get interested in this thing called the national identity? I keep asking myself. Why has it never been a preoccupation? Then I flash back to the parade of figures who encapsulate the New Zealander: The Man in the Street, The Kiwi Bloke, Your Average Joker, Joe Bloggs, Man Alone. They pass me by. Fenced off by language and image. Clearly the New Zealander is a white male, struggling to 'do it himself', pushing through the bush, hacking through the supplejack in search of his identity. Or maybe he wears khaki and has gone off to the battlefield. If he is an artist or poet, I see him leaning on a bar, drunkenly declaiming his philosophy of life. I wonder if you can have a New Zealand identity in a kitchen or at the clothesline. I wonder if you can have one on a marae.[7]

And, as James Jupp notes, in writing about the Australian context:

> There were obviously quite serious contradictions and tensions within the broadly egalitarian ethos that is often held to define the Australian national identity between the 1890s and the 1950s. 'Typical' Australians did not believe in the equality of women or of races and ethnic groups. They resented social inequality but equally

resented intellectuals who criticised such inequalities and sought social liberalisation.[8]

For our purposes, there is one further important cultural concern to note at this point and that is a particular preoccupation with the landscape. In both countries, though the geographic conditions vary enormously, the power of the landscape has proved irresistible over time and it returns again and again as a dominant and enduring image. As Rattigan notes, this struggle, this relationship with the land served (and may still serve) to underline the distinctiveness of life in Australia, to enhance its sense of separation from the rest of the world (especially Europe). It is a relationship that is important, too, to the indigenous peoples in both countries (Maori and Aboriginal) for both of whom the land has an eternal and spiritual significance.

The Present Moment
By the 1970s, fuelled by the civil rights movement and by feminism, some major shifts in consciousness were, however, under way in both countries. Maori nationalism was gaining momentum in New Zealand and in both countries, though with some different emphases, the role of the USA in the Vietnam War, Britain's entry into the EEC, the developing economic prowess of several Asian states were all giving new impetus to questions of national identity and helping to create a new assertiveness. Old myths and perceptions continued to find expression in a number of 'boys' films' such as *Crocodile Dundee* (Peter Faiman, 1986, Australia) (which contains both the aestheticised landscape and the hero as bushman/ocker) and *Goodbye Pork Pie* (Geoff Murphy, 1981, New Zealand) (an anti-establishment road movie which celebrates mateship and denigrates women), but increasingly, from the late 1970s onwards, another cinema was emerging too, the cinema which is the focus of this book. A particular set of funding initiatives and government policies in Australia and New Zealand, a particular political and social context, and some recognisable and much reworked images of cultural identity, have helped to provide the context for the creation of some distinctive films by women directors, who have worked or are currently working in Australasia. We shall be arguing that many of their films share a commonality of interest and approach and, in this book, we focus on three of their major preoccupations: the family, the landscape and ethnicity. The family is an especially strong preoccupation; here, as in the concern with

ethnicity, it is as if the film-makers were exploring the things that have always been omitted from the prevailing cultural myths, the absences, the experiences of the women as the mothers/wives/daughters of the down-to-earth, good, keen blokes. The dark side of the collectivity myth, the off-beat, the dysfunctional identity and the nuclear family are explored, notably by Jane Campion (in *Sweetie*, for example) but also by Gillian Armstrong (in *High Tide*) and Alison Maclean (in *Crush*). The romanticisation or the invisibility of indigenous peoples in their countries' cinemas is addressed through a preoccupation with ethnicity in the films of Merata Mita and Tracey Moffat; ethnicity is also explored to some extent by Armstrong (in *The Last Days of Chez Nous*) and Campion (in *The Piano*), as well as in a number of short films made by women in both countries. Lastly, landscape is a key motif in many of the films we shall be dealing with, including *My Brilliant Career* (Armstrong, 1979) and *Trial Run* (Melanie Read, 1984) for example, as well as *Mauri* (Mita, 1988), and it is not so much now a beautiful, touristic panorama that we find but more often a living, challenging and, at times, sinister presence which forms and changes the lives of those who dwell in it and engage with it.

These three concerns (the family, ethnicity and landscape) overlap and thread their way in and throughout the chapters that follow, each of which has a particular focus: on a key film, a director or a theme. We have chosen to concentrate on the fiction film (both features and short films) because it is such a rich vein to tap in terms of the radical representations of women that are available in such work. Our decision to include shorts as well as feature films (both independent and commercial) is based on our belief in the strong links between the two forms. Most of the female directors of the features in question have arrived via an underground or art school route, as did Jane Campion, for example, and the production of short films has been an important way into the industry for many women in both Australia and New Zealand. Notwithstanding the two countries' distinctive social, cultural and political identities, there has been a constant exchange of ideas and talent across the Tasman. In 1986, a co-production treaty was signed and, with New Zealand still lacking a major film school, the relationship looks set to continue. The films themselves are, of course, the proof and in this book we argue that many of them have a shared approach, particularly to the three major concerns identified above.

This is not to say that there are not some differing national emphases, too; a number of New Zealand women film-makers, for example, have produced work which is most aptly described as psychodrama, with a distinctive feminist tilt, while Australian women film-makers have seemed more preoccupied with suburban family dysfunctionality, again viewed from a female perspective. The New Zealand feminist psychodrama is closely allied to the psychological thriller but has distinctive narrative twists and a heightened preoccupation with gender, especially gender confusions and conflict. It emerged as a film form in New Zealand in the early 1970s and remains a dominant genre there, among women film-makers particularly. The Australian concern with suburban experience and with young girls growing up in damaging families, for example, is also interwoven with concerns about gender and sexuality, as well as (increasingly) ethnic difference.

There are other films made by women in both countries which we have not included; the book is not intended to be a definitive account of all such films and does not include discussion of some very worthwhile documentaries, for instance, or of animation films by women. And our selection of features and shorts is unashamedly partisan; most are drama-based and all are films which we have enjoyed immensely. They are films which have something to say, to women viewers in particular, about the kinds of experiences women have (in families, for instance, or as members of particular ethnic groups), experiences that have been neglected by much mainstream film-making. In foregrounding these concerns, New Zealand and Australian women directors, whichever country they have been working in, between them have created an impressive and highly specific body of work which is worthy of close attention from academics and serious film-goers alike.

2

Brilliant Beginnings

My Brilliant Career (Gillian Armstrong, 1979) was the first major feature film to be directed by a woman in Australia for over forty years[1] and it came at the end of a decade which marked the revival of the Australian film industry. Looked at within that context, it may be seen to share many of the preoccupations of what has come to be known as 'New Australian Cinema'. This wave, which began with a number of state subsidised films in 1970, represented a renaissance, not only in Australian cinema but also in Australian nationalism, and dealt with questions of national identity and the cultural mythology underpinning it. The declared agenda of government film funding via the Australian Film Commission, at least in the first decade of the revival of a national cinema, was to put Australia on the screen and to encourage the production of quality films. The feature films of the 1970s more than fulfilled this aspiration, nationality and landscape being the key preoccupations.[2]

Picnic at Hanging Rock (Peter Weir, 1975) represents something of a prototype of the Australian preoccupation with landscape. It is a period film which deals with the enigma of four schoolgirls who go missing during their school geography trip into the bush on Valentine's Day 1900. Its painterly compositions and use of natural light to create a lyrical but uncanny atmosphere are emblematic. So, too, is the subject-matter, dealing as it does with the relationships between young women. Two years later, in *The Getting of Wisdom* (Bruce Beresford, 1977), we return to the repressive atmosphere of a Victorian girls' school in a female rites-of-passage film.

My Brilliant Career shares many of the preoccupations of these two films. It is a period piece, set in the years 1897–1901, in which the protagonist, Sybylla Melvyn, a young woman brought up in the bush, attains knowledge and success in her quest to be 'an artist', through her continued and forthright rejection of the roles available to women at the time.

Compared to its precursors, *My Brilliant Career* is a more overtly feminist film, not least because of the strong female input at the level of production. Of the eight principal credits, six are women: screenwriter, Eleanor Witcombe; production designer, Luciana Arrighi; costume designer, Sue Armstrong; associate producer, Jane Scott; producer, Margaret Fink; and director, Gillian Armstrong. The film's links with the themes of Australian cinema (landscape, the pioneer and the cultural realities of turn-of-the-century Australia) are unquestionable. It is distinguished from other such films, however, by its clear connections with the international women's movement of the 1970s whose refrain 'Why be a wife?' is one wholeheartedly endorsed by the central character, Sybylla.

Neil Rattigan, in his book *Images of Australia*, observes that the enduring legend of the pioneer from small farmer to more affluent squatter provides the scope for centring the narrative round a woman, since it is women, he argues, who are granted 'considerable status', frequently even pride of place.[3] Within this legend, it is often women who are considered central to 'cultivation' and it is they who are thought to have a 'civilising' effect. This is shown to be the case in *My Brilliant Career*, which consequently proves fertile ground for exploring women's roles and their survival mechanisms in the face both of great hardship and relative wealth. This legend is also examined in Helen Grace's short film *Serious Undertakings* (Australia, 1983).

The character of Sybylla foregrounds the struggle of the personal; within the diegesis, her book pays tribute to the struggles of her countrymen and women. As such it is a feminist film rooted in Australian cultural politics. It is, in fact, the first Australian feminist film.

Literary Antecedents

Notwithstanding its essential Australian characteristics, *My Brilliant Career* owes a strong narrative debt to *Jane Eyre*, the nineteenth-century, English, pre-feminist novel. Sybylla's book and Charlotte Brontë's book, both written in the first person, chart their growing development in the face of social hardship during the Victorian period. The parallels are underlined in both their romantic encounters and unwelcome positions as governesses. Both are seen and see themselves as plain but clever. The motor of their respective narratives is the struggle against an unjust situation resulting from the inferior status assigned to women in society. This is experienced as a personal lack of power: no money, no means. Sybylla is informed early on in the film that she is to be placed as a servant; in her mother's words, 'We can't afford to keep you any longer.' Like Jane Eyre, Sybylla is very 'spirited' and resists her richer relatives' attempts to marry her off. Her aunt says, 'Marriage gives us respectability', to which she replies, 'That's what men want us to believe'. The alternative is unthinkable or, at best, bleak. Aunt Gussie says to her, 'Loneliness is a terrible price to pay for independence', but Sybylla continues to question the matriarchy. The film's ending shows Sybylla rejecting marriage with Harry, in spite of the affection (and 'mateship') between them. Ironically, at this stage he is no longer 'a good catch' since he is about to forfeit his property to the bank and become a poor man. This, however, is not Sybylla's reason for refusing to marry him; it is her fierce desire for independence and a career.

The film's resolution was a source of disappointment for romantically-inclined audiences – but that, of course, is the point. Jane Eyre settles for marriage, albeit a love marriage and highly unconventional. Brontë's heroine is of her time and there is no other choice except marriage or loneliness. Sybylla is a representation of the film's own time, addressing the issues of 1970s feminism; she is not to be so easily recuperated. In a sense, the film sacrifices verisimilitude to make a contemporary personal–political point: Why be a Wife?

Cinematic Influences
While it is the nineteenth-century English novel that provides a cultural reference point for the feminist underpinnings of *My Brilliant Career*, it is classic Hollywood melodrama of the 1930s and 1940s that shapes it discursively. It is not unusual to find the films of the New Australian Cinema adopting the generic conventions of commercial Hollywood movies. Australia's national cinema, in its 1970s incarnation, had to address the twin demands of a 'quality' cinema that would deal with specifically Australian themes and the commercial requirement that the films do well internationally. As a result, the films of this period are balanced between 'art-house' and commercial – a familiar dilemma for many national cinemas. In this case, what tends

to happen is the grafting of specifically Australian stories on to popular generic structures, albeit adapted and modified to some degree. Thus we have *Razorback* (Russell Mulcahy, 1984), described as highly reminiscent of *Jaws*, a psychological thriller; *Gallipoli* (Peter Weir, 1981), a war film described as the Hollywood (formulaic) 'buddy' movie; and *Mad Max* (George Miller, 1979), a full-blown genre film, a cybo/psycho/sci-fi thriller which was critically acclaimed as outdoing Hollywood. Inevitably enough, the generic influence most identifiable in *My Brilliant Career* is the melodrama, in its sub-classification as the 'women's picture'. Critically defined in terms of the centrality of its female characters, its *mise-en-scène* and its drama based in repression within the site of the domestic, it is easy to see how many elements of *My Brilliant Career* conform to this genre. It is interesting, too, to note how very adept Gillian Armstrong became at working this genre both at home and in Hollywood.

The 'women's picture', a dominant generic form throughout the Hollywood of the 1930s and 1940s, was frequently a 'period' piece, often set at the turn of the century.[4] The female character was invariably the central point of interest and the setting was, more often than not, the close domesticity of the home. The films were thus involved in representing the repression that underpinned family life, as well as in exploring a number of possible conflicts (to do with generation, gender and class). *My Brilliant Career* exploits this rich cinematic legacy, while dealing additionally with a specifically Australian cultural and cinematic preoccupation – landscape and land. As such, its central oppositional structure is 'culture' versus 'nature', drawing both on generic conventions and specifically Australian themes.[5]

Nature versus Culture
The dominant critical approaches to Hollywood melodrama are in terms of *mise-en-scène* and stars. *My Brilliant Career* was instrumental in creating two stars of the New Australian Cinema, namely Judy Davis (Sybylla) and Sam Neill (Harry). Since they were not stars at the time of the film's production, they cannot be seen to carry the iconographic power of a Bette Davis or a Franchot Tone. Consequently, the most productive approach to *My Brilliant Career* is in terms of its *mise-en-scène*. The central opposition of 'nature' versus 'culture' can be located within the iconography of the Australian landscape

film and the Hollywood melodrama respectively. Visually this translates as:

Outside	versus	**Inside**
Long shot		Mid-distance/close-ups
Space/empty frame:		Cluttered frame:
trees, animals		framed photographs, piano, ornaments, rocking horse
Workmen		Women

There is a further sub-division within the diegesis between:

Poor/small farms versus **Large affluent 'squats'**
e.g.   e.g.
(i) Sybylla's parents' place, called Possum Gully
(ii) The McSwats' (the outback small-holding where Sybylla works as a governess).

(i) Sybylla's grandmother's place, called Caddagat;
(ii) The Beechams' farmstead, called Five Bob Downs (where Harry lives).

With respect to the first and most fundamental opposition within the diegesis, the opening sequence of the film is illustrative. It begins with a long landscape shot. Barely discernible within the space is Possum Gully, small, insubstantial and drought-ridden. We move to a closer shot of the house and we see, from the outside looking in, Sybylla at the window, putting the finishing touches to a letter in which she describes herself, in voice-over, as egotistical but unashamed. This is the starting point of the novel (presumably epistolary in form) which she is to have concluded by the end of the film. We cut to inside the room and hence have a reverse shot, from the inside looking out. A dust storm is blowing up; small figures, farm workers, are struggling with cattle and with the weather which is becoming ever more wild. Sybylla, in voice-over, is discussing the importance of music, art and literature while, around her, laundry is taken off the washing line and windows are being firmly closed. The relay of a shot-reverse-shot, from inside looking out to outside looking in, works to establish visually and very powerfully the opposition between outdoors and indoors and Sybylla's position in terms of it. She remains throughout quite static and untroubled (almost unaware) as the storm rages around her. Her well-modulated voice contrasts with the howling wind, barking dogs and mooing cows. We conclude with Sybylla that she does not belong in this world; even inside, she is out of place, as the next sequence shows.

This is the living room. The camera pans from framed photographs on the piano to the space which the rest of the family occupy. Apart from the father who is collapsed in an armchair (presumably exhausted by his arduous day), the remainder of the group, mother and children, are engaged in industrious and practical activities: stoking the fire, sewing, doing homework and so on. By contrast, Sybylla at the piano appears irresponsible, flippant, inappropriate, unproductive. When her mother asks her what kind of job she imagines she can do, she replies, 'Writer or pianist' in high-falutin' tones. In the next sequence, which is a brief one-shot sequence of her parents in bed, we hear the well-spoken (English) mother expressing despair about her eldest daughter. In a broad Australian accent, the father replies, 'Same as all your damned family – delusions of grandeur.' The father's demeanour and clothing suggest a rough, down-to-earth, real (Australian) man. He is set implicitly in contrast with Frank Hawden, the English 'jackeroo' (or novice), a guest at Sybylla's grandmother's place, who is meticulously dressed, with waxed moustache and affected expression – an English wimp.

Sybylla is sent to Grandma Bossier's residence, a much more affluent 'selection' (as such farmsteads were known). We learn that Sybylla's mother has married beneath her and is consequently living a life of penury compared to the rest of the family, at Mrs Bossier's, including Uncle J J and Aunt Helen.

The visual contrasts between Possum Gully and Caddagat represent a fundamental division between a colonial and a much more authentic Australian settlement. This is underlined through the decor of Caddagat, with its (English style) servants, formal dinners, silverware and crystal, all of which is in stark contrast to the small farm Sybylla has left behind. Moreover, this new world or space is shown as more feminine; with the exception of Uncle J J who comes and goes intermittently, it is inhabited and dominated by women – and one fastidious, very feminised English guest. Initially, Sybylla believes she has found her real space. She has earlier remarked to her sister Gertie that she has no intention of living out the rest of her life in the bush (Possum Gully). She says, 'I might as well be dead', adding that work and sleep

BRILLIANT BEGINNINGS/15

Sybylla (Judy Davis) takes on Harry (Sam Neill) in *My Brilliant Career*
Still courtesy of BFI STILLS, POSTERS AND DESIGNS

are the only two states of existence there. It does not, however, take long for Sybylla to realise that she is also out of place at Caddagat. Her wildness of spirit, her strong will and her refusal to make a good marriage place her at odds with this cultivated, feminised and constrained world.

Wild versus Tame
This new opposition between the 'wild' and the 'tame' is visualised in the film through a number of contrasting sequences and represents the film's engagement with the notion of national identities, of Australia versus England. Sybylla's attempt to live the feminine life ('Learn to cultivate feminine values,' says her aunt) begin with her working on her appearance, skin, hair and clothes. This is followed by a strongly marked pastoral scene: Sybylla with parasol next to an ornamental lake, reading a novel with gloved hands, the perfectly refined young lady of Victorian portraits. Frank Hawden arrives with a floral tribute, which she graciously accepts until his back is turned, at which point she tosses the flowers into the lake. This moment of animation coincides with the rains arriving and Sybylla abandons her ladylike pose and stands exalting as the rain pours on her and soaks her to the skin – a vision of wild and wayward abandon. This shift from tame to wild is repeated visually throughout the film: there is a formal dinner at her grandmother's followed by what her grandmother subsequently describes as 'a Bacchanalian debauch' where Sybylla entertains the menfolk with lewd pub songs and dances suggestively with Frank. Similarly, when Harry Beecham takes her out in a punt on the river, the mood is initially sedate. Sybylla describes the atmosphere as 'English' and she recites poetry. Then, with a wicked gleam, she upsets the boat and both she and Harry topple into the water, much to Sybylla's glee.

Sybylla's wild gleefulness of spirit is increasingly tempered not by the civilising attempts of the matriarchy (Aunt Gussie, Aunt Helen, Grandma Bossier) but by her realisation of the poverty and hardship of those less privileged than herself. It is during feeding time in Aunt Gussie's aviary that Sybylla remarks how much more fortunate are these birds, having food and water provided daily, than many of her countrymen who are forced by drought and other hardships to take to the road and beg. In fact, by the time she has accepted the invitation to stay at Aunt Gussie's and Harry's place, Five Bob Down, Sybylla has acquired a measure of self-knowledge and compassion. She is also well aware of the contradictions of her position. She cannot survive in the bush, she cannot survive in the constraints of the more affluent farmsteads. She will not marry. Even her romance with Harry is premised on an equality rather than a conventional courtship – they are 'mates'. They have pillow fights and play piano duets together in which Sybylla refuses to take a secondary part, asserting herself as Harry's equal at every turn and initiating the communication between them. She continues to maintain that having a career, not marrying yet still being happy is not 'an impossible dream'. Her learning curve is completed when she is forced to become a governess to a small farmer's unruly and unkempt family, because her father owes them money and is unable to pay. Her resolution and strong will prevail over the chaos and she is able to 'civilise' the children by teaching them to read, so providing them with a sense of self-esteem and increased quality of life. Realising the parallels between the hardships of life at the McSwats' and her parents' existence, she is able to return to Possum Gully with a measure of humility and with her debt to them paid. She has, however, lost none of her drive to pursue a brilliant career, so while helping with the daily round of life in the bush, she is able to complete her novel, which is finally published in Scotland.

As remarked above, her final rejection of Harry's offer of marriage, the resolution of their romance, is made from a position of strength, confidence and self-knowledge. She understands that her marriage to Harry would destroy him and she has never deviated from her early avowal: 'The last thing I want is to be a wife out in the bush having a baby every year.'

The style and pace of *My Brilliant Career* serve, like the narrative development and *mise-en-scène*, to articulate and express the diegesis in a lyrical, fluid and seamless way. Many of the compositions, both of characters against a landscape and the more formal set pieces, the ball, the social occasions, are extremely painterly and frequently breathtakingly beautiful; the finely observed detail of the interiors and the sweeps of vast stretches of sky and land seem to be based upon contemporary paintings. The pace of this film, like *Picnic at Hanging Rock*, is often languid, yet it is always Sybylla, central in narrative as well as in visual terms, who provides the movement and energy, driving forward (often literally) into uncharted territory. She at once encapsulates the spirit of the Australian pioneer and of feminism and it is Sybylla who in a sense represents the starting point, prototype and role model for many of the strong female representations that were to follow. It could be argued that the recurrent visual motif of Sybylla at the piano finds its apotheosis much later in the film *The Piano*, Jane Campion's stunning study of female determination.

3

A New Zealand Landmark

Melanie Read's film *Trial Run* (1984) was billed as the first feminist feature produced in New Zealand. It is a deliberate and provocative attempt to rework an established genre (the psychological thriller) along feminist lines and to revisit and revise the roles conventionally assigned to women in such films. It overlaps, too, with the domain of the Hollywood horror film, and to some extent with the science fiction film, in concerning itself both with 'unnatural' or supernatural events and with the uses and abuses of technology.

Thematically, the film evidences a strong concern with the land and the natural order as well as with women's experiences of the family; in these ways, it is typical of the Australasian women's wave. The landscape is here, as we shall see, not just a picturesque backdrop but a major force to be reckoned with, hostile to intruders and animate almost, in ways that are strongly reminiscent of *Crush* (directed by Alison Maclean) which was to appear some eight years later. The preoccupation with family is also strong and Rosemary's role as wife and mother, as well as (critically) her relationship with her son, are key themes. Her domestic and familial situation is clearly etched; in fact, as finally revealed, it is her positioning and status as a mother that has led to her torment.

Local Context
As well as making reference to established Hollywood genres, as might be expected *Trial Run* also picks up on some features of its own local cinematic context. In its treatment of landscape, noted above, the film refers to and departs from local convention. Landscape had hitherto been much celebrated in the national cinema with

documentary films setting the style early on. From *Romantic New Zealand* (a feature-length government travelogue released in 1934) to *This is New Zealand* (a three-screen Expo promotion film made in 1971), the country has celebrated its stunning and spectacular landscapes, and nowhere have these films been more popular than in New Zealand itself. The majority of New Zealand's feature film-makers have also dwelt on and engaged with aspects of the land, and have of course been encouraged to do so by the Film Commission's sponsorship requirements. Nevertheless, what Melanie Read describes as 'the predilection for the whole glorious rural NZ trip'[1] may well have other roots too, and while the special relationship that many Maori have with the land is acknowledged, there is in addition a kind of fascination in the country with tourism, with travel, a deep pride in the beauty of the place that finds expression in the cinema, as well as elsewhere. Increasingly, a shift has been occurring, however, from the use of the landscape as little more than the inevitable backdrop (to an equally inevitable car journey) to films such as *Crush*, *Vigil* (Vincent Ward, 1984) and *Trial Run* itself where landscape begins to exhibit a life of its own, even a spirituality, and where human relationships with the land become themselves the subject of scrutiny.

Other local considerations affected the production, too. It took Read three years to get NZFC funding for the project during which time she made *Hooks and Feelers* (1982), a 50-minute drama based on a short story by Keri Hulme. She had previously completed several documentaries. For her first feature film, Read had wanted an all-women crew for the production but in the event had to settle for 23 women out of a total crew of 33. This compares well with the majority of New Zealand films, where usually only 20 per cent of the crew is female. Read both wrote and directed the film and ensured that the female input was felt; key crew positions held by women included the production manager (Eloise McAllister), unit manager (Margaret Hilliard), production designer (Judith Crozier) and art director (Kirsten Shoulder). The music was by Jan Preston. Similarly, the majority of the supporting roles are taken by women. The key character, Rosemary (Annie Whittle), is surrounded by independent and effective women; the roles of the publisher, the estate agent, the tractor driver and glazier, the police officer and the close friend (Frances, played by Judith Gibson) are all taken by women.

The Run as Central Motif

The film's first few opening sequences introduce its key concerns. From a classically romantic seascape at night, we move quickly inland and indoors to a remote farmhouse, where the orange morning light filters eerily through billowing curtains, to the accompaniment of indeterminate sounds – a rustle, perhaps waves on the shore, a tinkle, and a plaintive, recurring theme. This landscape is suddenly less natural than supernatural, with a force and life of its own. The tourist's peaceful panorama has been displaced. The film cuts to the outdoors again, and in the yellow dawn three runners appear in the middle distance, their feet beating a rhythm on the ground.

The run will become the central organising motif of the film. It is an activity Rosemary shares with her two teenage children and it provides a focus for the family in their interactions with each other. Running is not a liberating experience for them, however. It gives James (Christopher Broun), a computer-obsessed adolescent, an excuse to control his mother, to dictate her diet and details of her training schedule, and to demonstrate the superiority of technology. He has complete confidence in the computer's ability to assist his mother to victory in the forthcoming cross-country event.

Running is a source of friction in the family. As the camera slowly circles the family dinner table, the warmth and intimacy of the setting (it is James's birthday) are undermined by the open expression of hostility between brother and sister and between father and daughter. Anna (Philippa Mayne) is openly critical of her brother's reliance on the computer and is accused by her father of being jealous of James's achievements. This family, far from being drawn together through a shared ambition (for Rosemary to win the race), are in open rivalry with each other. There is a cut then to the empty farmhouse at night, and to the sound of running feet. A ghostly female figure appears in the blue half-light. Throughout Rosemary's ordeal in the remote farmhouse, the sound of running feet will return, just as her family keep returning, to reconstitute themselves and their tensions.

As a competitive athlete, Rosemary is physically strong and mentally independent. A successful wildlife photographer, she is offered a new commission to photograph the rare yellow-eyed penguin, a job which will mean living near the bird colony on the coast for six months. Her family react in various ways to the news: husband Michael (Stephen Tozer) is supportive ('We can manage here'), James is resentful ('Mothers don't go on holiday for six months'), and her daughter

Anna thinks they ought to be paying her thousands more and that it is unreasonable to have to work every day 'just to do a chapter'. Rosemary defends her decision staunchly; she is not doing it for the money, it is not just a chapter and she won't be having a holiday. Family tensions are evident again, with Anna (inclined to support her mother and to defend her from James's criticisms) finding herself again under attack from her father.

Having committed herself to the project, however, Rosemary is determined to stay in the farmhouse. Running is again the motor for the narrative; Rosemary runs to the coast with her binoculars to locate the penguin colony and to the phone box on a time trial; later, she runs to Alan West's (Martyn Sanderson) farm to challenge her taciturn neighbour to keep his dog on his own property. Thus the film's narrative space is established, the terrain clearly mapped out.

Natural and Unnatural Worlds
When Anna and James visit, they go for a cross-country run with their mother, as in the opening sequences of the film, not a leisurely, relaxing run but a competitive, technical affair, timed and orchestrated by James. The running takes them through and across the rural landscape; they are clearly intruders into the natural order with their technology and their competitive interests.

The natural world increasingly comes to life for Rosemary. As she returns to the cottage, after learning that Mrs West died there, natural sounds are mixed with unnatural ones; she looks up and a low angle shot of the huge trees towering overhead, black against the bright daylight, suggests her increasing unease. In her isolation, Rosemary is unsure how to respond to and account for events. The wood pile could have been disturbed by an animal but the flowers were cut down with scissors. How could a huge branch detach itself and hurtle through the air from the cliff top, missing her by inches? What animal or bird could produce such frightening and unnatural nocturnal noises? It is a landscape that comes to life, as it were, and one which embodies a clear threat.

Rosemary's attitude to her natural surroundings differs sharply from Alan West's. While she seeks to conserve and protect the wildlife, to photograph and document, he is detached, unconcerned, for example, about the preservation of penguin nests on his land: 'That'd be the Wildlife Services' job, not mine.'

Thus an early tension arises (a familiar one in the New Zealand context) between those who are seen to exploit and appropriate land for their own uses and those who would strive to defend and protect the rights of its indigenous inhabitants. Rosemary and her friend Frances go to some lengths to keep Alan West's dog away from the penguins, even injuring it in the process; unlike the penguins, the dog is not a native but an intruder and there is a sense in which all intrusions here, even Rosemary's with her camera, create an unease and threaten to unbalance a natural harmony. The ordinary and remote rural world of the farmer, his dog and the tractor driver, is not ordinary at all but sinister and unpredictable.

Photography is used, thematically and visually, to highlight this disjuncture. Still photographs evoke the past for Rosemary: her children playing when they were younger, her relationship with Michael, her friend Frances's relationship with Michael. Early in the narrative, as she prepares to leave for the cottage, the photographs serve to substantiate a past, to validate a sense of the ordinariness of family life, of the things she will miss. Later, her own photographs of the penguins are violated by an unknown intruder. Snapshots of Frances with Michael disturb her and appear to suggest betrayal and a photograph of Rosemary as she stands on the beach, moments after a branch has hurtled from the cliff towards her, suggests the presence of an observer with malicious intentions. Unlike the others, this is a photograph which was not (could not have been) taken by her. As tension builds, photographs change from being mementos and snapshots of natural and happy events into omens, their very stillness and unnaturalness highlighted, their relationship with reality now in doubt.

This opposition between the natural and the unnatural is picked up, too, by James's obsessive dependence on the computer; every run must be analysed and outcomes calculated; he puts long hours into the task, alone in a computing laboratory at night, reluctant to leave – and even his leisure time at home is spent playing computer video games.

Family Betrayals
The regular visits by Rosemary's family to the cottage serve to underline her positioning as wife and mother and effectively to re-position her; she cannot, it seems, move away from them altogether. When Frances also visits, Rosemary hugs her in genuine delight. There is a warm

bond, too, between Frances and Anna: 'How's my favourite Amazon?' asks Frances. The strength of the women's relationship with each other is clear and Frances stays with her friend in the cottage to offer reassurance and support.

Frances is, however, an ambivalent presence. She is strong and loyal but she has an independent lifestyle and her dress code, her drinking, her face tattoo and her innuendos all mark her as 'deviant' in patriarchal terms. As mentioned, there are suggestions of a past relationship between Frances and Michael, and also suggestions of a possible sexual relationship between Frances and Rosemary. Even Rosemary seems to doubt her friend when she discovers her absent from the bed, moments after all the windows have been shattered. Frances is a 'femme fatale', in fact, a source of unease and disquiet in the narrative but, like Alan West and the tractor driver, who are also sinister presences, she serves finally to distract attention away from the real culprit.

The final sequences of the film are shot at night, and Rosemary is alone in the cottage. A hand-held camera circles the farmhouse, suggesting the presence of an intruder; the eerie unnatural noises begin again. Rosemary struggles to contain her fear, and her vulnerability is clearly underlined in the shots of her taken from outside the house. A strange object hurtles against the window, moments before Constable Miller knocks on the glass to see if Rosemary is all right. The reprieve is only temporary, however, the common-sense realism of the policewoman being immediately countered by an unnatural uproar of squawks and cries. The nightmare culminates for Rosemary in the appearance of James at the door, covered in blood and apparently on the point of collapse. When she is forced to run to the telephone box to call for help, a series of flashbacks to the many times she has made the run before, bring us full circle. The end sequences reveal that it is James who has become her tormentor, who has contrived an ordeal for her which would force her to run 'for her life' and achieve a record-breaking time in the process. The computer-obsessed teenager (so the flashbacks suggest) has built this terrifying spiral of events, culminating in his own feigned collapse, which would force Rosemary to perform as she had never done before, superhumanly. All the 'unnatural' and inexplicable events witnessed by his terrorised mother are laid at his door, in the final few sequences of the film. The spectator learns that the natural bond between mother and son has been, as it were, the source of all her terror. With the unveiling of the son as 'monster' and the clearing of all other suspected perpetrators, in a kind of inverted Oedipal drama, the film reaches its bizarre and extraordinary ending.

The motif of the run, therefore, acts as a structuring device for the narrative and it effectively serves to foreground the family as a site of repression and even cruelty. The teenager's obsession with technology has overridden all other more human concerns; a natural enough desire to help his mother succeed has escalated wildly and he has become 'unnatural' in his persecution of her.

James's relationship with his mother is, in fact, the final enigma of the film. Far from providing narrative resolution, the ending of the film opens up question after question, about the real nature of the relationship between James and his mother, about success, envy and competition in families, about the impact of technology and culture on the natural world. The only riddle that has been solved is the identity of Rosemary's tormentor.

Reworking the Psychological Thriller

The role of woman as victim has become central to the psychological thriller. Hitchcock's film *Psycho* (1960) is probably the best known of the genre and it inspired a cycle of such films in which mythical monsters were abandoned in favour of protagonists with more conventional sexualities; a deliberate, self-conscious engagement with Freudianism began.[2] In *Psycho*, the male and female characters are locked in a struggle for dominance which culminates in the notorious shower sequence where Marion becomes fixed as an object of both the male look (that of the audience and the protagonist) and of direct physical attack. Characteristically, the woman in the psychological thriller is in peril, in danger of her life and the subject of (in modern times) increasingly vicious attacks, often sexual ones. As noted elsewhere,[3] in *Psycho* the situation is complicated by Marion's transgressions (she is not passive but active and she becomes a thief in order to secure what she wants) and by Norman's sexual ambiguity. Although clearly established as a male protagonist, when he kills he is part mother and part son, and suffering from a pathological condition supposedly stemming from an early betrayal and his murder of his mother years before.

Unlike most psychological thrillers, in *Trial Run* it is never really a question of whether the female victim would survive or not; Rosemary has experienced betrayal, intrusion and abuse as well as violence, but

Rosemary (Annie Whittle) in peril in *Trial Run*
Still courtesy of BFI STILLS, POSTERS AND DESIGNS

despite her paranoia and fear, she stands firm and remains capable of action in moments of crisis. Feminist interest in the psychological thriller has focused on gender relations and has seen the tendency to objectify and victimise women as representing a male desire to punish and constrain women's sexuality. In psychoanalytic terms, this desire arises from the fear and the threat of castration which is embodied in female sexuality for the male subject.[4] Within this framework, these films can be read as catering for a male audience's unconscious wish to see the woman bodily destroyed and the threat which she represents thus allayed.

Trial Run refuses its viewers the opportunity to engage with it in these ways. We are given a woman 'in peril', in danger of her life, but we are not given a helpless victim and we are not given the images of vicious bloody attack or of unrestrained violence against the female body. Our 'victim' is a strong woman who despite intimidation, violence and threats survives a life-endangering situation and stands firm and physically undamaged finally to confront her tormentor. There is therefore a deliberate mismatch between certain aspects of the Hollywood psychological thriller and the film *Trial Run*.

In making the strong woman both victim *and* protagonist, however, a difficulty is created for the viewer. She is the film's key player, the independent narrative lead who must solve the mystery and, in this way, the suspense is defused. The film is finally more of a detective's puzzle, a 'whodunnit', and the tension associated with the psychological thriller, so much of which is generated through the chase and through identification with a victim, is finally absent. *Trial Run* successfully explores women's responses to violence, intrusion and betrayal, both within the family and the landscape, and it does so in positive, non-stereotypical ways, but the eliding of the roles of victim and protagonist creates a paradox in narrative terms and effectively restricts the viewer's involvement. In ending (rather than beginning) with an enigma, the film does offer a challenge to the nature of narrative itself and, in giving us a strong female victim, it challenges the nature of the male audience's expectations. In portraying strong women and a strong contemporary female friendship, as well as a strong mother-and-daughter relationship, the film is essentially feminist. As psychological thriller, however, although it contains all the signs of a thriller (the steady accumulation of fear and menace, supernatural goings-on, a haunted house), it is finally undercut. The psychological thriller conventionally addresses a male audience and in removing the mechanisms and the strategies for this mode of address, *Trial Run* is finally at odds with the genre, not so much working *in* that mode as *about* that mode.

A year later, in 1985, Gaylene Preston was to complete *Mr Wrong* which, like *Trial Run*, was also billed as a feminist thriller. The film shares many of the same concerns, has a female victim/protagonist, and addresses the subjects of fear and sexual violence. Its heroine is young, more vulnerable, less consistently strong and less aware than Rosemary, and the threat to her is more directly felt, more physically demonstrated. Her attacker is visible, his intentions ultimately plain; she escapes with her life, partly due to her own resourcefulness but also with the assistance of the ghostly Mary Carmichael, to witness the violent destruction of her tormentor. As a consequence, *Mr Wrong* in fact sits much more comfortably within the thriller genre; there are fewer obstacles to the audience's identification with the female victim, and narrative expectations of the genre are satisfied. Its subject-matter may be broadly termed feminist – female revenge is exacted and the themes of sexual violence and women's responses to it run throughout the film – but its form remains conventional. *Trial Run* is, on the other hand, an attempt to rework the very framework of the thriller genre itself.

The NZ Feminist Psychodrama

Through its experimental engagement with the form of the psychological thriller, Melanie Read's work has successfully foregrounded the gender component of the conventional genre and highlighted previously latent concerns with sexuality. In addition, its preoccupations with anxiety and fear, with the inner dreamlike world of the key female protagonist, put it clearly into the New Zealand psychodrama tradition. It is, in fact, an example of what we shall be calling the New Zealand feminist psychodrama.

According to Roger Horrocks,[5] what is known as 'psychodrama' in New Zealand film corresponds to a tradition in New Zealand fiction which was the main alternative to realism. As a writing genre, psychodrama emphasised dreams, fantasies, anxieties and inner conflict and it emerged clearly as a film form in New Zealand in the early 1970s with films such as *Threshold* (Richard Phelps, 1971).

Trial Run undoubtedly influenced later work; *Mr Wrong* was also important in this context. The short films *Kitchen Sink* (Alison Maclean, 1989) and *Time Trap* (Sally Smith, 1991) are two of the better-known examples of the feminist psychodrama that followed and *Sweetie*

(1989), which is Jane Campion's first full-length feature film, also draws on the same New Zealand tradition. The New Zealand feminist psychodrama, then, is closely allied to the psychological thriller but has distinctive narrative twists, is concerned with deep personal anxieties and has a heightened preoccupation with gender, often exploring gender confusions and conflict. We shall be referring to feminist psychodrama again, particularly in our discussion of short films.

In addition to breaking new ground in terms of its exploration of the thriller genre, *Trial Run*, as we have noted, also engages with cinematic representations of the landscape and with beliefs and attitudes in relation to the natural world. A decade later, in her film *Vacant Possession*, Margot Nash again interrogates notions of ownership and exploitation of the land and though the mood and style of this film differ greatly, some key preoccupations remain and recur, as they do throughout the Australasian women's wave. Another key preoccupation that we have noted here is women's experience of the family and this concern, too, weaves in and throughout many of the films we have discussed. In *Trial Run*, the narrative has a specific Oedipal inflection, as we noted, and the nuclear family is clearly identified as a site of unease, cruelty and repression. Despite strong female friendships and a strong mother–daughter relationship, the potential within the family for inflicting harm on its members is unambiguously signalled.

4

Short Circuits

In our exploration of women-produced, women-orientated film narratives, the short film represents an important phenomenon, not only because of its obvious link, via the film-maker herself, with the feature-length movie, but also in its own right, as a film form that has traditionally articulated (and continues to articulate) voices from the margins. The voices of feminists, women of colour and latterly of lesbians, speak through the short film.

Because of its undeservedly lowly status and the diversity of its origins and history, the short film is frequently neglected in books about cinema. In the Australasian context, however, the short film is impossible to ignore; it is an integral part of women's film culture.

In this chapter, we will be discussing a number of Australian and New Zealand shorts, from the early 1980s to the early 1990s, which exemplify the influence of the women's movement both in terms of women's issues and feminist theory, as well as highlighting respective national realities. These realities raise issues of the land, settlement, race, and urban or suburban existence and may be subsumed under the umbrella term of 'national culture'. In addition, we will be focusing on the development of particular filmic forms and highlighting shared themes and preoccupations. Clearly, this is not intended to be an exhaustive undertaking but rather to convey the flavour and scope of the Australasian short film tradition.

Background
Historically, women have entered mainstream film-making either through documentary or the semi-experimental drama. In the Australian and New Zealand experience, the short drama has served

both as prototype and as conduit for crossing over into the commercial sector, either through direct state subsidy or big budget private financing. The film-makers profiled in this book almost all trod this path, having emerged from no- or low-budget contexts which include film-making co-operatives, women's cine clubs and art colleges.

Although it is not our intention to focus in detail on the documentary tradition, it has to be acknowledged that this has been extremely important in providing fledgling film-makers with early production experience and a track record with which to enter the industry. For example, both Gillian Armstrong and Merata Mita have been involved in making documentaries.[1] We are, nevertheless, more interested in the thematic and stylistic links between short, often experimental film dramas and the subsequent feature films; in this chapter, therefore, we will be noting some of the links between the Jane Campion short *A Girl's Own Story* and her feature film *Sweetie*, and our discussion here of Alison Maclean's short film *Kitchen Sink* will be picked up later when we come to her feature film *Crush*.

The women's short film first made its impact in the early 1970s. This is not to suggest that women were not making films before this time but 1960s experimental avant-garde work did tend to be the province of white male film-makers. This is true not only of Australasia, but also of North America and Western Europe, where such films tended to be located within a male-dominated underground. Within the USA, which was the most powerful base for this kind of production, a few women did attain recognition in spite of the odds. Film-makers such as Maya Deren, Shirley Clarke, Marie Menken and Carolee Schneemann, while not always receiving the recognition they deserved, were nevertheless inspirational and provided an antidote to the critical canon of men's films that was beginning to dominate art colleges and museums by the 1970s. It is interesting to note that in 1973–74, when the Australian Film, Television and Radio School (AFTRS) enrolled its first students for the one-year interim programme, there was a reluctance to recruit women since, as one lecturer observed, they would end up as butchers' wives in the suburbs. Happily, Jane Campion was one of the students enrolled that year and a strong women's perspective became a hallmark of the school.[2]

At all events, by the mid-1970s in both Australia and New Zealand the women's wave was gathering momentum. This was the result of two key influences, the first being the impact of the international women's liberation movement, the second being the establishment in both countries of film-funding bodies whose brief was to support and finance a national film culture. In Australia, the two major sites for independent short film-making were the cultural centres of Sydney and Melbourne. From the 1960s to the early 1970s, the women's film-making that did exist was tied either to the Sydney Film Makers Co-op or to the Avant Garde Film Making Group in Melbourne. Women associated with the co-op scene, who continued to produce avant-garde work throughout the 1980s, included Susan Lambert and Sarah Gibson, Corinne Cantrill (with Arthur Cantrill) and Jayne Stevenson (with Paul Fletcher). With the advent of feminism, Susan Lambert made a feminist action short *On Guard* (1983) and subsequently returned to a more subjective experimental mode with Sarah Gibson in the film *Landslides* (1986). The feminist influence became clear not only in the shifts in content of the co-op-based films but in newly formed groups associated with it. In 1973, for example, a women's film group was established in Melbourne called Reel Women. In Sydney, feminist film-makers formed the Sydney Women's Film Group. Funding was supplied by the Australian Film Commission via the committee known as the Women's Film Fund which lasted until 1988. AFTRS also became a crucial site for the production of women's films.

Similar patterns of funding were emerging in New Zealand with the setting up of the Short Film Fund and the Creative Film and Video Fund, both of which continue to this day. Although there was no national film school, there was no dearth of women ready and willing to make films and they formed small cine groups or worked out of other artistic and educational sites. Alexis Hunter, whose early feminist short *Anatomy of a Friendship* (1973) 'explored images of women in conflict with their own images of themselves', was a student at Elam art school in Christchurch studying sculpture at the time.[3] Gaylene Preston was also a student at art school when she began making films. It is worth noting here that these women, and others like them, do in fact reflect a familiar pattern in which women film-makers from many countries have often used film in the context of exploring other artistic media; for example, Maya Deren came from dance, Carolee Schneemann is a painter and performance artist and Tracey Moffat a photographer.

In New Zealand, as elsewhere in the embryonic feminist film culture, documentary was initially the preferred form. It was a relatively inexpensive and direct way for women to explore the social and political (as well as personal) issues thrown up by the feminist agenda. The first feminist documentary in New Zealand was Deirdre MacCartin's

Some of My Best Friends are Women (1975). Notable also for illustrating the concerns of women's documentary in the 1970s is Stephanie Beth's *I Want to be Joan* (1977), which explored women's attitudes to the experience of motherhood, and Shereen Maloney's *Irene 59* (1981), in which the film-maker's mother reflects on her various roles as a wife and mother from the perspective of an older woman who is beginning to discover her full potential.

Generally, though, by the mid-1970s, the explosion in women-made, women-orientated documentary was beginning to tail off. Other kinds of representations were being contemplated as confidence increased, funding held and interest grew. All this had been the direct result of the feminist network in which film-makers toured to talk about their work to a range of women's audiences, including small workshops and women's organisations, both social and political. There was, however, a new trend emerging in the 1980s, particularly in New Zealand, but also in Australia to some extent (as a number of New Zealand-born women moved to Australia to study and to work). This trend was the use by women of the film narrative form known as 'psychodrama'. Into this category we can place Melanie Read's *Trial Run* as one of the more popular examples of the genre. In fact, the psychodrama colours many of the most notable films made by New Zealand women, including Jane Campion, Gaylene Preston and Alison Maclean. *A Girl's Own Story*, *Mr Wrong* and *Kitchen Sink* are all, for example, variations on the theme.[4]

In order to provide a flavour of the range of work, we have chosen to discuss those films which share and illustrate specific concerns, in pairs. First, we want to look at two films which are informed by feminism (both in terms of activism and theory) whose range also incorporates the historical, political, social and artistic aspects of contemporary Australian life: they are *Serious Undertakings* (Helen Grace, 1983, 28 mins) and *Shadow Panic* (Margot Nash, 1989, 25 mins). Second, we will look at two films which illustrate how a number of different filmic forms can be used to explore the reality of female identity within the family. These are *A Song of Air* (Merilee Bennett, 1987, 23 mins) and *Swimming* (Belinda Chayko, 1990, 11 mins). Moving then to the New Zealand tradition, we want to examine two formative shorts by film-makers who have moved into feature-film-making, namely Jane Campion's *A Girl's Own Story* (1983, 26 mins) and Alison Maclean's *Kitchen Sink* (1989, 14 mins). Both films provide fascinating examples of the feminist psychodrama.

Feminist Foundations

Serious Undertakings provides a good starting point for looking at the feminist concerns and filmic preoccupations that were characteristic of women's semi-experimental work at that time. It is a critically acclaimed film and it won the prestigious Rouben Mamoulian Award for the best short film of the Sydney Film Festival in 1983. The film invokes certain Australian cultural myths and is structured around two typical and traditional examples of the artistic enshrinement of those myths, namely a short story by Henry Dawson called *The Drover's Wife* and the famous triptych painted by Frederick McCubbin called *The Pioneers*. Both narratives, literary and visual, celebrate the landscape and pay tribute to the heroism of the bushmen. But, notably, both works of art represent the women, the wives of the bushmen, as strong, active subjects, crucial to the family's survival, rather than as appendages or victims. To some extent, both representations, and obviously the film itself, challenge the masculinised version of Australian land settlement as sexist and inaccurate. Women, it seems, have always been active partners with men in the reality of the outback. To underline this, we hear a girl's voice reciting Dorothea Machellar's patriotic ballad *The Wide Brown Land*: 'I love a sunburnt country...'[5]

Serious Undertakings is an experimental film and has no linear narrative or dramatic development. It is divided into five parts, or discrete elements, which relate only obliquely to each other. Each part uses a different (or a number of different) filmic devices to construct its meaning. So, for example, part 4, which deals with Australian intellectuals discussing the family, is filmed in the style of a documentary film with 'talking heads'. Part 1, which is concerned with the role of the mother as political activist, can loosely be described as 'suspense film', using the devices of a thriller. The final part uses Soviet montage techniques as an allusion to radical film history.

The film is a highly analytical piece of work. As well as presenting a complex image of the state, its exploration of female being is rooted in a commitment to history and materiality. Its central concern is to interrogate the relationship between female identity and certain cultural representations. This is reminiscent of issues which are central to Gillian Armstrong's film *My Brilliant Career* but, in terms of its formal strategies, *Serious Undertakings* is much more radical. It is much more a film essay than a drama and it leans heavily on the works of 1970s theorists, including Kristeva and Barthes, both in terms of its discursive approach with the use of structuralist and psychoanalytic

The pram as an icon of activism in *Serious Undertakings*
Still courtesy of CINENOVA

language, and in terms of its filmic strategies which are self-reflexive and function to deconstruct the notion of a stable or fixed meaning.

One of the film's projects is to expose the mythology, rooted in Australian ideology, of egalitarianism and anti-authoritarianism, and, in the process, to expose flaws in the arguments of the liberal intelligentsia. In one notable sequence, the method used is the deconstruction of the filmic image itself while four male theorists (and one co-opted female) discuss aspects of feminist discourse. During this sequence, both the sound track and the image track are progressively disintegrating; a sharp comment, as it were, on the reliability of the arguments being put forward. Sylvia Lawson, in her essay on *Serious Undertakings*, describes the techniques: 'By transformed video devices, the images are colour separated, turned abstract, recomposed and then as it seems permitted to disintegrate.'[6] In fact, there is a range of deconstructive devices in the film and it is not always easy to watch or follow, but, as the title suggests, it has serious intentions.

Drawing (just as seriously) on traditions of anarchism and surrealism, as well as on revolutionary feminism, Margot Nash's *Shadow Panic* deals – albeit in a completely different way – with many of the same issues as *Serious Undertakings*. This ASIF (Anarcho-surrealist Insurrectionary Feminists) Production, written and directed by Nash, with cinematography by Sally Bongers (whose visual flair provided the characteristic 'look' for a number of Jane Campion's films), is an experimental drama which is poetic rather than prosaic, emotional rather than theoretical but which deals, as does *Serious Undertakings*, with the relationship between cultural mythology and female identity.[7]

Like *Serious Undertakings*, *Shadow Panic* does not work in a conventional narrative way. There are three very loose story lines which are focused somewhat enigmatically around the exploits of three unconnected female characters. Each of the three protagonists represents something of an archetype. There is the dreamer (a red-headed woman), the investigator (an Aboriginal woman) and the hot head (or fool), a young woman who dresses stylishly and drives fast cars. Nash's approach is to mix a kind of urgent realism (the Aboriginal woman is tracking a corrupt capitalist who is involved in shady land deals) with a kind of dreamlike surrealism. For example, the dreamer is preoccupied with her memories of childhood and her love of natural beauty. This latter story is filmed in a flowing and poetical way. The fool, who is a kind of catalyst to the connections between them, at least structurally, as she finds herself walking into or driving through the other two narratives, is represented in a way as female potential; she becomes powerful once she casts aside the distractions of romantic love. Together they might even be described as representing the relationship between the conscious and the unconscious – the ego, the super ego and the id.

Shadow Panic has been described as 'a film about internal and external states of emergency, about personal and collective shadows' and Margot Nash herself states:

> Making *Shadow Panic* was an experiment in structure. By working only with fragments connected via the gaze, via chance, by shaking up narrative expectations, I hoped to create an atmosphere where the poetic, the fantastic could find expression. I wanted to work with the unconscious, not with logic, to create images that might resonate later much as a dream might.[8]

In terms of both its style and its preoccupations, *Shadow Panic* has strong links with the North American avant-garde, particularly with the films of Maya Deren.[9] But as well as being poetic, Nash's film is also very directly political. The respective characters' particular preoccupations, with childhood, with greed and with desire, form a whole in the struggle for female survival against the patriarchal, capitalist assault on legacy, land and life.

Both *Serious Undertakings* and *Shadow Panic* therefore, in very different ways, represent critiques of patriarchy, in its repression of female energy and the female subject, and of capitalism, in its exploitation of the land. *Serious Undertakings* reinstates women in relationship to the land and celebrates their work as active partners in the settlement process, and *Shadow Panic* connects the political and personal struggles of women to the land via the motifs of sea, earth and sky. Both films owe a debt to feminist and revolutionary theory and both are extremely effective.

Mothers and Fathers

Narrowing the horizon somewhat from nationhood and landscape to personhood and family, the next two films to be discussed deal with family life from a daughter's point of view. Like *Serious Undertakings* and *Shadow Panic*, Merilee Bennett's *A Song of Air* (1987, Australia) received funding from the Women's Film Fund of the Australian Film

Commission and it was given a special mention at the Cannes Film Festival in 1988. The film uses family photographs and excerpts from a number of 16mm home movies, made by the film-maker's father during her childhood, to trace her development from girl to woman. In this sense, it is a female rites-of-passage film.

Bennett's strategy in *A Song of Air* is to reclaim and thereby reconstruct the images from her father's films by adding her own voice over them. In this way, she guides us through the strict (conservative and Methodist) regime of her life and, in so doing, draws a portrait of an Australian middle-class family in the 1950s and early 1960s. Her father's version of family life, as evidenced by the home movie footage, presents an idyllic picture: seaside holidays, romps in the garden, every family member knowing their place, father as initiator and breadwinner, mother nurturing and domestic, brothers chopping wood and fishing, sisters playing with dolls and puppies, a happy and trouble-free unit, church on Sunday, family round the table with father at the head. It is *his* charismatic image that Bennett's voice-over commentary focuses on. In *her* film, it is her female subject position that guides the narrative. In *her* version, the implicit repressiveness of this patriarchal institution is uncovered. Her childish adoration of her father is problematised as she grows into adolescence. Her voice (in the present) reveals her torn feelings for him, the enigmatic figure who has so shaped her life: 'I look at these pictures of my father in 1937. He was 29. I don't recognise him. There's only a young man I never knew.'

She follows the narrative through from pleasure to pain, unlocking both her desire and her hostility, noting how a young woman's subjecthood is constrained and denied in such a structure. The footage is moving and poignant, snapshots of a way of life gone for ever, containing the sadness of loss and the pain of memory: 'To find my own vision, I had to reject yours and test myself and find out what I was made of. Out of love you tried to prevent my pain but your safety is like suffocation.'

In this seeringly honest autobiography, Merilee Bennett shows that, in breaking her chains, she had to break away from her father. Alienated by the pain of separation, she moves to the city into a self-discovery which involves drugs and prostitution. Years later, she returns to visit the family, a liberated woman, but the process has involved personal pain, self-abuse and ultimately great loss; she is never fully reconciled with her father. Her voice speaks to someone who is

Family photograph in *A Song of Air* with father (Arnold Lucas Bennett), mother (Nancy Bennett) and infant (Merilee Bennett)
Still courtesy of CINENOVA

no longer there. The film is a lament, to the image of one who is absent; it is a 'song of air'. The enigmatic nature of film itself is contained in this sense of emptiness; this is its philosophical point, and its personal message is that, for girls, the patriarchal law of the father is deeply repressive and the punishment for disobeying it is loss of Eden and of innocence.

Another kind of loss, this time the loss of the mother, is the subject of Belinda Chayko's remarkable film *Swimming*. It is 11 minutes long, at least half the length of the others we have discussed already and, unlike the others, it was made at AFTRS. Shot on 16mm but using principally video and some Super 8 constructed home movie footage as its source material, its structure is much more elliptical than *A Song of Air*. Like that film, though, it expresses the emotional experiences of a young girl growing up in a nuclear family. In this case, the family is the suburban working-class unit, with some occasional remnants of the extended family, including an aunt and grandfather. The film is set in the 1970s and as such, superficially at least, the family regime is much more relaxed than that of the 1950s. The young female who is the central character possesses a portable video camera and the family scenes that she records with it provide the main imagery for the film itself. In spite of these differences, the central emotional experience of the young woman is similar to that of Merilee Bennett's persona in *A Song of Air*. As Belinda Chayko has stated about her own film: 'It's a film about feeling, not about knowing.' We are the spectators of the girl's video and, like her, we never really know what is happening or has happened. She is humoured and ignored by turns, so that the mystery of the absent mother is never quite resolved. There is a sense of concealment which is partially uncovered when the girl (and the video camera) sees what she is not permitted to see: the moments that suggest her mother's death. This is counterpointed by the sporadic intercutting of the Super 8 footage, which works, in home movie terms, to represent the missing mother. This footage is a crucial clue and the emotional core of the film. In it, a woman tenderly cradles a child; the same woman is seen on holiday, swimming in a pool. We, the audience, are swimming too, flailing about in our efforts to make sense of the visual clues to the girl's emotional reality. These moments of memory are enigmatic and represent a structured 'absence' in the film. The most important moments for the girl with her video are the moments that are unspoken, those which cannot be expressed. Her video recordings are both humorous and terrifying. As Adrian Martin has observed:

> These scenes are assembled in a deliberately fragmented, elliptical way, punctuated by violent glitch edits and finally coming to seem like the ambiguous 'testament' or audio-visual document of a young girl who has uncovered a terrible truth about her own family.[10]

The 'terrible truth' is finally the family's denial of the girl's need to know. As in *A Song of Air*, the parent who is the real subject of the film is no longer there (except in home movie images), and the loss and the pain are all the more moving for being represented only by their visual traces.

Short Psychodramas

The next two films we want to consider are the work of two New Zealand film-makers, Jane Campion and Alison Maclean, both of whom were able to secure financing for feature-length movies on the basis of successful short films. As a student, Jane Campion attended the Australian Film, Television and Radio School, where she made all her early short films. Alison Maclean, however, stayed in New Zealand and studied at Elam, moving from sculpture to film. According to Bridget Ikin, at Elam 'there was no support at all. They had a 16mm wind-up camera, that was it. She [Alison] was even printing her own negative.'[11]

Both *A Girl's Own Story* (Jane Campion, 1983) and *Kitchen Sink* (Alison Maclean, 1989) are quite distinct in mood and visual style from the Australian shorts discussed above. In terms of their genre, their procedures and preoccupations, however, these films are both unequivocally New Zealand shorts, representing as they do fine examples of feminist-inspired psychodrama. The mood is very dark and unsettling, almost surreal, and the concerns are with exploring taboos around sexuality and desire. Stylistically, they share a 'look' since they are both filmed in black and white. *A Girl's Own Story* is a student film, made on a low budget and shot on 16mm film. *Kitchen Sink* received financial assistance from the New Zealand Short Film Fund and is shot on 35mm.

The inimitable decentred visual style that so distinguishes *Sweetie* (1989) can be seen in the earlier Jane Campion film. In both films, the cinematography of Sally Bongers seems to capture visually the very texture of uncertainty and insecurity which is a feature of Campion's narratives, most particularly through the techniques of framing and composition.[12] The lighting, decor and cinematic codes (camera angle, distance and movement) are, in *A Girl's Own Story*, perfectly attuned to the subject-matter of the film which is about a young girl growing up in a dysfunctional family. This is a family which exudes repression and is not dissimilar to the one depicted in *Swimming*, where children are rendered invisible through lack of communication. As a result, each family member inhabits her or his own private world. The domestic space which they occupy becomes a strange and alien place. The mother is virtually mute with depression, the father is in deep denial and the sisters are hostile and prickly.

Of *A Girl's Own Story*, Campion remarks: 'I was interested in sexuality, in innocent responses commonly considered perverted. I wanted to capture the strength of teenage feeling, the aloneness of adulthood, the strangeness and strongness of family.'[13] Areas that Campion explores in *Sweetie* are touched on almost as a dress rehearsal in *A Girl's Own Story*. Subjects such as sibling incest, child abuse, clinical depression and obsessiveness are the staples of Campion's films. The family is represented as a site of moral danger and thwarted emotion; in *A Girl's Own Story*, the atmosphere is conveyed through the motif of cold (absence of warmth), with heaters that are never switched on. Characters speak in non-sequiturs and desire is clearly a sin. The convent, to which a girl made pregnant by her brother while they were playing 'cats' retreats, is a cold, bleak and secret place; these are the consequences of a Christian morality based on the 'word-of-the-father' and the admonition 'thou shalt not'. The girls' friendships are perhaps the only positive thing about the situation they find themselves in and there are some strange moments which are both moving and amusing. For example, in the opening sequence of the film, four girls (with tennis racquets for guitars) sing the Beatles' song 'I Should Have Known Better', so encapsulating, in one brilliant visual stroke, both the mood and period of the film. Later, two of the friends practise kissing, in a heterosexual role play, one playing the boy and wearing a George or Ringo paper mask, the other lying on the bed passively, playing the girl. The implicit critique here of gender roles and gender positioning within the nexus of the family is a central concern of Campion's and one that returns in her subsequent feature films.

SHORT CIRCUITS/**43**

'I Should Have Known Better', Pam (Gabrielle Shornegg), Stella (Geraldine Haywood) and Gloria (Maxine Knight) in *A Girl's Own Story*
Still courtesy of BFI STILLS, POSTERS AND DESIGNS

Akin to *A Girl's Own Story* in its visual darkness and strange camera angles and distances is Alison Maclean's *Kitchen Sink*. Its psychodramatic elements draw on the horror genre rather than the melodrama (as is the case with Campion) but it is closer to the body horror films of the 1980s than to the psychological horror of, for example, Melanie Read's *Trial Run* which also contains features of the thriller genre. Almost in the spirit of a reaction to feminist orthodoxy, Maclean's film draws on the tradition of films such as *Repulsion* (Roman Polanski, 1965) and the films of David Cronenberg in which desire and sexuality are encoded in terms of disgust, fear and loathing. Maclean confesses to her perversity: 'When I was growing up, I had an aberrant interest in bad girls. I despised my niceness.'[14]

The fundamentally misogynist nature of the whole sub-genre of body horror films is turned on its head by Maclean who, in this film, locates the basic horror in the site of the male body, and not the (castrated) female form which is its traditional location. Maclean's version of embryonic life, in which a woman pulls some increasingly grotesque thing out of the plug hole, is both outrageous and courageous. She continues her assault on the politically correct when fear and loathing in the kitchen turn into defoliation and desire in the bedroom; with the help of black plastic bin bags and razorblades, the female character constructs a man. Maclean's imagery is dangerous and deadly; shot alternately in unsettling close-ups or disorientating long shots, the film's denouement involves a return to the point of departure. The woman embracing the man feels a bristle extruding from the base of his neck; she goes to pluck it, and pulls and pulls . . . we hear a scream on the sound track and the cycle begins again:

> *Kitchen Sink* was . . . wanting to do something cinematic, to really learn about telling a story just using pictures, using *cinema*. I like films that do many things at the same time, or have a mixture of tones, so you don't know whether to laugh or . . . scream. It's one of the things I liked about *Sweetie* so much, that you can't quite get your bearings because you never have a chance to be comfortable.[15]

Both Campion's and Maclean's films are very accomplished, thematically and technically, dealing as they do with murky desire and Oedipal drama within the domestic sphere. While the preoccupations of women's documentaries from the early 1970s may seem a long way away, there is in fact a link. The political issues that the women's movement raised around female subjectivity, sexuality and gender practice are re-expressed here in the films of both women. As we shall see, the legacy lives on into their later work and is a testament to the more liberational and rebellious aspects of feminism. This spirit is also evident in *Shadow Panic*. It is a spirit of questioning and a refusal to sit down, keep still and be quiet, a refusal to behave or conform, even to the expectations of feminists themselves. In Alison Maclean's words: 'I seem to be drawn to [topics] that are uncomfortable, areas that feel unsafe for either men or women . . . I'm interested in exploring the ambiguous, contradictory side of sexual politics.'[16] It is also present in the attitudes of a number of female characters within the films where it is manifest as a refusal to allow the repressive mechanisms of patriarchy (whether as nation or family, whether in the bush or in the kitchen) to crush the female spirit. The films discussed above all bear strong testament to this spirit and all share and celebrate the potential of women to liberate themselves.

5

Other Identities

Recent films by indigenous women from Australia and New Zealand make exciting viewing. This cinema has been slow to emerge and slow to gain recognition but the process that Merata Mita calls 'decolonising and indigenising the screen'[1] is under way, especially in New Zealand, and the products of the process are distinctive.

The films selected for discussion here are two Australian short films, *Nice Coloured Girls* (1987) and *Night Cries* (1989), both made by Tracy Moffat, and a feature film called *Mauri* which was made in New Zealand in 1988 by Merata Mita. In various ways, these films pick up the themes of the family, ethnicity and the land that we have observed in many other Australasian women's work but there are now some distinctive emphases. Indigenous peoples in both countries are striving to free themselves from the dominant culture's perceptions and misperceptions, to make films which are distinctly and uniquely their own, to establish cultural sovereignty. Not surprisingly, ethnicity and racial difference, the relationship between white and black cultures, both in the past and in the present, are key preoccupations here, but there are also images of alternative or extended families and of distinctive relationships with the land, particularly, for example, in *Mauri*. Further, as we shall see, there are innovative attempts to challenge some of the dominant modes of film-making, the structures of narrative film itself, as well as the images and perceptions held by the dominant culture.

The Context
To contextualise the work of indigenous women film-makers, and to understand their current concerns, we need first to trace briefly the

development in both countries of a cinema that focused on the indigenous people, concerned itself with them to a greater or lesser extent and made them objects of the camera's gaze. For years, both Aboriginal and Maori peoples have endured (alongside other repressions) a kind of cinematic bondage. Barry Barclay describes it:

> Imagine as a whole culture not being able to talk about your own land in your own way. Imagine if you were born in London or Copenhagen, and the only – and I mean the only – images of yourself were scripted and shot by people from Algeria or Tamil Nadu and transmitted simply to capture good ratings amongst their own viewers.[2]

In fact, some of the earliest images of both indigenous peoples are to be found in ethnographic films made by the European colonists. The films of James McDonald, for example, which were made in New Zealand between 1919 and 1923, provide a valuable and rare record of traditional aspects of Maori culture and are now regarded as 'taonga', or cultural treasures. Though there is little evidence to suggest that these films were ever shown to their subjects at the time, in a unique and innovative move, and following an extensive archive preservation programme which was completed in 1986, the films have now been screened among local people, as an acknowledged way of returning the images to the tribes and areas from which they were taken. Merata Mita describes the audiences' response:

> It is not uncommon for archival screenings to be complemented by an appreciative living sound track of laughter, exclamations of recognition, crying, calling out and greetings. Even without the descendants and in a theatre, those participating become aware of the fact that they are privileged to share in rare moments of power and performance. Because what the audience sees are resurrections taking place, a past life lives again, wisdom is shared and something from the heart and spirit responds to that short but inspiring on-screen journey from darkness to light.[3]

By about 1912, the fiction film was becoming established and European film-makers in both Australia and New Zealand turned readily to the new form. In fact, fiction films of a significant length seem to have been made in Australia several years before they became common elsewhere.[4] In 1912, in New Zealand, the Frenchman Gaston Méliès made some short, romantic dramas which were all Maori, including one based on the love story of Hinemoa, and the first NZ feature film, which was made in 1914, was also called *Hinemoa*. In 1926, the story was again reworked, this time by a Danish director, Gustav Pauli, who produced *The Romance of Hinemoa*. This romantic fare was, of course, symptomatic of the persistence of a particular set of stereotypes (for example, the exotic, dusky maiden) and the films served to confirm audiences' expectations of life in the romantic South Seas, as well as their cultural ignorance. Other significant films with a Maori focus were a romantic drama set against the New Zealand wars of the 1860s called *Rewi's Last Stand* (which Rudall Hayward made initially as a silent film in 1925 but remade with sound in 1940) and *Broken Barrier* (John O'Shea/Roger Mirams, 1952) which tells the story of a love affair between a Pakeha (white New Zealander) and a Maori, the barrier being the racial divide that few New Zealanders were at that time willing to acknowledge. With this later film came a slightly grittier, more unsettling representation of New Zealand society and, despite the film's romanticism, it was an important statement which broke new ground.

The first Australian feature film to give Aboriginals a central place in the narrative was *Jeddah*, made by Charles Chauval, which appeared in 1955. Like *Rewi's Last Stand* and *Broken Barrier*, it too was made from a white male perspective but for the first time Aboriginals were not on the margins of the story as colourful or exotic foils to the exploits of white colonists. The film gave expression to a painful aspect of Aboriginal experience, namely the enforced adoption of their children by whites. This painful cultural memory is one which returns time and again and it has been expressed even more powerfully since in the work of Aboriginal film-makers themselves, for example Tracy Moffat. Thematically, *Jeddah* is a film about assimilation and it drew heavily on the discourses and debates of its time. Its characters embody a range of different perspectives in the debate, with Sarah (the white adoptive mother of Jeddah, the Aboriginal girl) characterising the belief that Aboriginals could be and should be assimilated, 'tamed' and brought round to a white lifestyle. Her husband, on the other hand, is more prepared to respect Aboriginal culture as distinct and meaningful in its own terms but, as Karen Jennings notes in her insightful book on representations of Aboriginality and gender, his paternalism is of a different form and he may be said to subscribe to a geneticist and essentialist view of the primitiveness of tribal Aboriginals.[5] The film's messages are mixed but it was important at the time it was released and it remains important, not least for its willingness to engage with such ambiguity and complexity in its representations of Aboriginality. Like the New Zealand film *Broken Barrier*, which was made a few years earlier, *Jeddah* was an important attempt to confront and explore some of the majority culture's deepest fears and suspicions about the indigenous people.

Throughout the 1970s and 1980s, the cinema of both countries continued to draw on a range of stereotyped images of their indigenous peoples and to express, with a greater or lesser degree of awareness, various attitudes towards difference. Australian feature films such as *Walkabout* (Nicolas Roeg, 1971), *Eliza Fraser* (Tim Burstall, 1976) and *Storm Boy* (Henri Safran, 1977) emphasised variously the Aborigine as alien, as primitive and non-white or as noble savage. *The Fringe Dwellers* (Bruce Beresford, 1986) had a more personal and particular focus, with no significant white roles and a greater concentration on individual characterisation. However, as Jennings argues (in a chapter entitled 'Individualising Difference'), it thus deflected attention away from the broader social and political questions of its day. In fact, despite being produced some thirty years later, it can be read, she writes, as an endorsement of a 1950s' assimilationist ideology.[6]

To Love a Maori (directed by Rudall Hayward) was released in New Zealand in 1972, a film described as a documentary-drama feature with 'a sincere bicultural stance'.[7] On the whole, however, at this time Maori were largely absent from the screen or were there simply on the sidelines (as in *Goodbye Pork Pie*, made in 1981 by Geoff Murphy), as part of the picturesque landscape or as caricatures (as in *Came a Hot Friday*, made in 1985 by Ian Mune). The romantic preoccupation with Maori people, and women in particular, that was a feature of the early cinema mentioned above, seemed by the 1980s to have diminished. The film *Pictures* (Michael Black, 1981) dealt with racial prejudice and some of its consequences, and *Utu* (Murphy, 1983), a kind of Antipodean western, confronted the issue of Maori land rights and the effects of colonisation. *Other Halves* (John Laing, 1984) and *King Pin* (Mike Walker, 1985) were both acknowledged as having addressed the urban experiences of young Maori with a degree of seriousness and concern.[8]

All of these films were, however, made by white film-makers and, increasingly, activists on both sides of the Tasman were becoming weary and dissatisfied with such portrayals of the indigenous cultures. It was becoming clear that the images themselves were not the point; the majority culture controlled the technical process of film-making and the voices of the minority were not being heard. The argument raged ceaselessly about the images and the perspectives (whether assimilationist or essentialist, whether progressive or regressive, whether 'fierce warrior' or 'noble savage'), and the indigenous peoples remained disenfranchised. Until they were in a position to make their own films, despite the obvious sincerity of many white film-makers, nothing would really change.

Indigenous Documentaries

The breakthrough in New Zealand came in 1974, with the television documentary *Tangata Whenua* (*The People of the Land*) which was written by Michael King (Pakeha) and directed by Barry Barclay (Maori) from Pacific Films. The series is described by Russell Campbell as being the closest New Zealand documentary had ever come to a discourse originating from within the Maori community[9] and, in its approach and style (long takes, no Pakeha 'experts' interpreting events), it was undoubtedly formative. Then, in 1980, the Australian Broadcasting Commission showed a documentary film called *My Survival as an Aboriginal* which like *Tangata Whenua* was also the product of a collaboration; Essie Coffey, an Aboriginal woman, wrote and directed the film with assistance from Martha Ansara and a white crew. The film is didactic in tone. Jennings writes:

> It is a committed, partisan statement, in which Essie denounces European dislocation and exploitation of Aboriginal people, and celebrates Aboriginal affinity with the land and a future of survival, dignity and freedom. Essie presides over *My Survival* as a matriarch.[10]

As noted elsewhere, documentary film-making has often provided a way into the mainstream industry for marginalised groups, and this has been no less true for indigenous film-makers. In New Zealand, in 1983, Merata Mita's documentary film *Patu!* was released; it traces the growth of the anti-apartheid movement in the country prior to the 1981 tour of the South African Springbok rugby team and does so from a Maori perspective. The film created almost as much controversy as the tour itself. In drawing a parallel between a racist South Africa and a Pakeha state which was prepared to go to extreme lengths, putting its police in riot gear for the first time ever, in order to preserve links with the apartheid regime, Mita struck at the heart of New Zealand society.

Through television and through documentary, indigenous filmmakers like Mita and Barclay were gaining experience and expertise. Some technical training schemes were set up for Maori, such as Kimihia, the comprehensive training scheme run by Television New Zealand in 1989 with funding from the Maori Affairs Department. By this time, Barry Barclay had completed the first Maori feature film *Ngati* (1987) and shortly afterwards came Merata Mita's feature *Mauri* (1988) which was the first to be made by a Maori woman. The first feature to be made in Australia by an Aboriginal woman was *Bedevil*, directed by Tracy Moffat in 1993 and described by her as 'funny, scary and terribly arty'.[11]

This, then, is the specific context. Both countries have a history of making films about indigenous peoples, from the ethnographic and historical to the paternalistic, the socially concerned or the demeaning; as indigenous people have themselves started to take control, to put themselves behind as well as in front of the camera, the films have started to change and the representations have shifted significantly. We consider these shifts now in the work of two indigenous women, Merata Mita and Tracy Moffat, who are both actively exploring new modes of address within the medium of film; both have a dual project of investigating identity, ideology and history within their respective cultures and of drawing attention to the means by which our understanding of such issues is constructed.

Nice Coloured Girls

Moffat's short film *Nice Coloured Girls* (1987, 18 mins) focuses on relations between white men and Aboriginal women. Such relationships were conventionally seen in terms of dominance and powerlessness; the white European male was the predator and the Aboriginal woman was typically presented as a virgin or a whore, or (to use the phrases found in eighteenth-century ships' journals) as a 'shy maid' or a 'wanton strumpet'. But Moffat's view is different. These orthodox categories are rejected in a film which, as Jennings notes, celebrates 'the perceptiveness, ingenuity, skills and sexual power of Aboriginal women in white Australia'.[12] It is not a straightforward reversal of roles, however. Although on one level the film is 'about' three 'coloured girls' who take revenge and fleece a white 'captain' during a riotous

The aboriginal ancestor (Rosemary Meagher) in *Nice Coloured Girls*
Still courtesy of CINENOVA

night in downtown Sydney, on another level, a number of anti-realist or experimental devices are employed which effectively prevent us from reading it so simplistically.

For one thing, the film moves back and forth through several spatial and temporal zones. The opening visuals, aerial views of downtown Sydney at night, are accompanied on the sound track not just by the noise of traffic but also by the sounds of a rower and oars dipping; text appears superimposed on the night city scene; it is an extract from a ship's journal from 1788 which gives an account of an Aboriginal woman's approach to the side of the colonists' boat. Clearly, we are to be engaged in a re-contextualising of historical experience and understandings.

Mismatches between sound and image persist throughout the film. A male voice reads from a ship's journal as the three young women walk through the city, the hand-held camera conveying a feel of direct experience. This sense of personal history or biography is reinforced by the next sub-titles which read like extracts from the young women's diaries and then by cutaways to the sea shore, to a medium shot of an older Aboriginal woman, a relative or ancestor perhaps. Snatches of Aboriginal language, women's laughter and the sounds of waves accompany the night-club scenes, where the 'heist' is in full swing, and then we cut to a still, a painting of an early colonial scene. The camera pulls back to reveal a gilded frame and then, as if to stress the constructed and two-dimensional nature of this image too, a white male arm reaches across in front of the painting dangling a small purse of money. A black woman's arm reaches out for it.

A few shots later, a similar symbolic device is used again; a rope ladder falls in front of another still image, this time a portrait of a ship at anchor. Sounds and lights of the city accompany the image and a male voice reads aloud from an early settler's journal which describes how some Aboriginal women could be enticed to spend the night on board a ship; a male hand reaches down from the top of the frame to beckon and assist, and four young Aboriginal women climb up the rope ladder and disappear from view.

In another metaphorical sequence, images of a white fist smashing the black glass over a painting of Sydney Cove are intercut with scenes from the night-club hoax. Green paint is sprayed over a white hand laid on black skin, leaving a stencil imprint, an indelible mark; then a black hand with a spray can reaches across and sprays black paint over the front of another early settler's painting. History can be rewritten; its false images and constructions are being revisited and revised. They can be wiped out.

Nice Coloured Girls has been compared with *Serious Undertakings*, discussed earlier. Both films set precedents within the context of feminist film-making in Australia and both were influential. *Nice Coloured Girls* explores the limitations of familiar dichotomies such as white/black, oppressor/oppressed, attraction/repulsion and past/present. But it also engages with the nature of representation itself and effectively questions the constructions, the language and perceptions of the majority culture in relation to history and identity.

Night Cries

In Tracy Moffat's *Night Cries* (17 mins), made two years later in 1989, her photographic training and background is once more extremely evident. This short film was made with support from AFTRS, the Department of Aboriginal Affairs and the Australian Film Commission. It is visually stunning and mesmerising to watch. It is (perhaps with deliberate irony) subtitled *A Rural Tragedy* and, like *Nice Coloured Girls*, it attempts an exploration of the nature of relationships between the indigenous and the colonising races, this time on a more personal level.

Set in a studio landscape, a space without depth or perspective, washed in rich, artificial colours, without dialogue, the film takes us beyond language, as it were, to memory and to our earliest experiences of dependence and power. It opens with an Aboriginal evangelical singer, singing about communicating with Jesus. An Aboriginal daughter cares for an elderly white mother in her dying days; she feeds her, wheels her to the toilet, washes her feet. We assume she is a foster mother and that the film-maker is alluding to the adoption of black children by whites in Australia, during the days of assimilationism. The film may therefore be read as exploring some of the political and emotional legacies of this practice from a black female perspective.

The presence of both races within one relationship raises political issues which are underlined as the camera focuses on the paraphernalia of tourism and colonisation (photographs, a suitcase, a travel brochure). But the photographs have personal meaning, too, and together with old footage of a family seaside holiday they manage to evoke a past in which a young black girl was dependent on her white mother for protection and care. The mother's absence created panic and fear, a sense of betrayal. Now, in her senility, the mother's very presence provokes rage and disgust, impatience and bitterness. As the film's emotional intensity increases, the sound track disintegrates and the gospel singer mouths his now voiceless platitudes; religion (another legacy of colonialism) is an empty promise.

In the final sequences of the film, the elderly white mother lies dead on the ground; beside her, curled like a foetus, lies her middle-aged black daughter, shaking with grief – but it is a young child's crying that we hear on the sound track. Cries heard in the night carry across the ages; in this highly stylised and evocative film, sound is dislocated from its image, just as the present may be dislocated from the past.

Past displacement is also the subject of another recent short film from the AFTRS called *Terra Nullius* (21 mins) which was directed by Anne Pratten and made in 1992. Anne Pratten spent several years working with Aborigines and Torres Strait islanders. She is herself Aboriginal by birth and, like Tracey Moffat, she was adopted and brought up by whites. This experience provides the focus for *Terra Nullius* which is made from a child's point of view (rather than from the perspective of the older Aboriginal woman, as in *Night Cries*) though there is here, too, an attempt to trace the accumulative effects and the meaning of cultural displacement over time. *Terra Nullius* is an Aboriginal child's search for identity. It has a particularly memorable final sequence in which the child, kneeling on a windy beach, is enclosed by a circle of Aboriginal women; the women face inwards at first, drawing around the child protectively, then they turn outwards, as if to ward off danger; finally, one of the women kneels with the child and slowly, tentatively, reaches out to her. There is here, in this conclusion to the film, an affirmation of the importance of community and of its positive, healing potential, in contrast to *Night Cries* where images of isolation and pain persist to the end.

Mauri

Community is also a key theme in Merata Mita's first feature film *Mauri* (or 'life force') which was made in 1988 in association with the New Zealand Film Commission. The film uses many inexperienced and non-professional Maori actors and was shot by a largely Maori film crew. Despite an elliptical narrative, it is in fact 'all of a piece', a fluid and organic exploration, from a Maori perspective, of what it means to be Maori in twentieth-century Aotearoa New Zealand. Here, as in *Ngati*, Pakeha are the outsiders, the foils in a Maori-centred story; they are the spectators and the transgressors.

The opening sequences of the film allude succinctly to its major preoccupations. A Maori is making a long-distance telephone call from Auckland; angrily, he corrects the operator's anglicised pronunciation of his name; rapidly, we cut to the interior of a dark room where a fire is burning and a telephone ringing; it is the middle of the night and an elderly Maori woman enters the frame in her dressing gown, holding a lighted candle; she reaches for the telephone; we cut immediately to another candle-lit room where Rewi (Anzac Wallace) lies on his bed, fully dressed; he starts at the sound of knocking and, as he reaches for a gun, we see a brief flashback of a white car rolling over a cliff at night. Rewi makes for the door clutching his gun; in the half-light, he opens it to receive the woman Kara (Eva Pickard) who has news about the phone call. The rain is lashing down outside. Next, we cut to the corridors of a hospital; Maori are gathering for a birth. At this important moment, the community is drawing together; the Pakeha doctor in his white coat is a bemused bystander as Maori supervise; when he is asked to help, he calls for a scalpel but Kara gives him a sharp shell-like object. 'Use this; this cut the cords of generations,' says Kara. She refuses to let the doctor dispose of the placenta. 'The afterbirth is part of us,' she says and the next shots show the ceremonial return of the afterbirth to the land.

In this brief footage, lasting little more than two minutes, the film's key concerns have been mapped out: the rhythm of the life cycle, the inextricable bond between the people and the land, the significance of community, the value of acquired wisdom and the importance in all things of a cultural perspective. Rewi's spiritual disquiet, his nightmarish flashbacks, have set up a narrative enigma but this narrative is not just about an individual struggle to come to terms with a past; Rewi's lack of spiritual integrity also has an impact on the community; his struggle is their struggle, too.

The Pakeha characters continue (like the doctor at the hospital) to look in from the outside; Steve Semmens (James Heyward), a young Pakeha man who was brought up locally, is reminded that he should know better than to intrude; his demented and racist father (played by Geoff Murphy, director of *Utu*) openly spies on the community through binoculars. Pakeha politicians, with their inept pronunciation of the language, their cultural insensitivity, and their refusal to listen and learn, are figures of fun; they, like the old Mr Semmens, occupy an irrational position, as it were, in the context of the film's thematic. Such ignorance, it is suggested, can lead only to insanity or buffoonery.

Steve himself is respectful but, this time, it is Pakeha who must assimilate Maori ways; he must be willing to learn just as Awatea, a young Maori girl (played by Rangimarie Delamare) is willing to learn from her elders and her community; she watches but in silence and with an open mind; her looking will bring her wisdom.

As we see from the opening sequences, Rewi is haunted by a bad memory, by the knowledge of a crime he has committed; until a resolution is found, he is not free to be with Ramari, Kara's niece (played by Susan Paul), as lover or husband, and not free to be at peace with his people or himself. The approaching death of Kara, the matriarch, near the end of the film, provokes his confession. 'Death has a way of calling out the truth in all of us,' she says. His crime was not murder but the stealing (as it were) of another's identity. Following a fatal car accident, he took the personal effects and the identity of the man he had been travelling with and he returned, as an imposter, to the dead man's community. He is not her nephew Rewi at all; he belongs to another tribe and in taking another man's identity he has broken more than Pakeha laws: 'The shadow of the dead man overtook me until my world was too dark to live in.' The dying Kara tells him he must go to where the dead Rewi lies and ask forgiveness; if he succeeds, he can be a full man again, if he fails he will die.

'Rewi' is now a fugitive not just from Pakeha justice but from his community and himself; scenes of his anguish are intercut with shots of a gathering thunderstorm and, on the far side of the river, in the haze and the middle distance, a tribal dance. This is his real betrayal, a betrayal of his history and his tribe; the warriors' chanting and the reverberating thunder signal his emotional upheaval; he must find a way to return, to become spiritually whole again. His eventual capture, on a high cliff overlooking the sea, at the scene of his crime, is intercut with Kara's death. Of the two Maori policemen who approach him, the older can only hold and embrace him; it is left to the younger more ambitious policeman, one who has already been established as a traitor to his culture and his history, to handcuff him.

This ending is made more apocalyptic still by Kara's death. Eva Pickard is a prominent campaigner in New Zealand for Maori land rights, and as Kara she is the elder, the acknowledged leader of the community, the repository of cultural wisdom, an earth mother and a spiritual healer. She teaches Awatea the traditional handicrafts and she reminds her nephew Willie (Willie Raana) of the proper way to approach a burial ground. She passes on cultural understandings about birth, death and life. And she has special intangible powers, such as a foreknowledge of Willie's death.

As a reviewer at the film's premiere noted, women in this film embody nothing less than destiny.[13] Ramari loves Rewi but cannot marry such a troubled man, even though she is pregnant by him; in the aftermath of Willie's death (at the hands of his own gang) she decides to marry Steve, as 'the best thing she can do' under the circumstances. As Bill Gosden writes, her actions 'absorb conflicting forces in her world and restore harmony to the land and the people'.[14] The community comes together in celebration and joy.

Mauri is beautifully filmed by cinematographer Graham Cowley. There are stunning images of the landscape throughout but perhaps most memorably in the final sequence, as Kara dies and Rewi's torment ends. A heron flies and the camera circles high, tracing the contours of the land above the tiny community; a low sound like wind gradually gives way to women's voices singing in Maori and a small girl, who has watched and waited and learned throughout, runs to the hilltop to wave farewell to Kara's departing soul. The camera circles and finally draws away, as if it is itself Kara's spirit in flight.

But the film is more than this, more than a moving expression of a vital and expansive culture. It is an active exploration of the structures of film, an attempt to find an appropriate form in which to tell the stories of a community. These are stories in which the community itself has centrality, rather than any individual character, and the film's narrative structure is correspondingly more diffuse, containing as it does a number of narrative resolutions within it (such as Ramani's wedding, for example). Here the process of telling may be more important than any one story itself.

In terms of genre, there is no easy fit either. At times, the film looks a bit like a western (there are campfires, a shoot-out, gangs, and episodes of honour and betrayal) but there are no stars and women are central. In many ways, this is a film about relationships, rather like a melodrama, but the nuclear family is replaced here by a more inclusive form of kinship, a network and a community. These more inclusive relationships, like the relationship with the land and with the past, are signalled in some highly symbolic ways (rather as they were in some of Tracy Moffat's work which was discussed earlier) so that with Rewi, in his pain, we see a tribal memory as it were, of warriors dancing by a river. Spatial and temporal verisimilitude cannot be assumed and these reworkings of a classic narrative structure, this de-emphasising of the personal and foregrounding of process and of relationship, make the film quite distinctive and easily one of most powerful and important yet to come out of New Zealand.

In many ways, the work of both Tracey Moffat and Merata Mita resonates with the work of other women we have discussed. For example, the relationship between a mother and her daughter that is at the centre of *Night Cries* is also central in Gillian Armstrong's film *High Tide* (1987); the adolescent 'rites-of-passage' theme from *Nice Coloured Girls* also surfaces in *A Girl's Own Story* (1984) by Jane Campion; and the sense of a living land that permeates *Mauri* is also present in *Trial Run* (1984) by Melanie Read, as well as in Campion's *The Piano* (1993). The work of the indigenous women, however, combining as it does an interrogation of issues related to both race and gender, and coming as it does directly out of the film-makers' experience of a double oppression, is noteworthy for its thematic intensity, as well as for its readiness to challenge the form and the mode of dominant representations.

6

Child's-eye View

The focus of this chapter is the prevalence of girl children and female adolescents in Australian women's cinema and, to a lesser extent, in New Zealand women's cinema, specifically in the films of Jane Campion. We will argue that not only are there many important young female characters in these films but also that it is their perspectives that are privileged in terms of the narratives overall. Here, we explore this particular element across a number of films (both shorts and features) and show how the young female point of view functions to shape the mood and meaning of the films in question.

This privileging of the child's (particularly the girl's) point of view seems to be a quintessential aspect of the Australasian women's wave. Australian national cinema generally, however, does include a number of notable productions which focus on both boys and girls. Among these are such distinguished titles as *Picnic at Hanging Rock* (Peter Weir, 1975), *The Getting of Wisdom* (Bruce Beresford, 1977), *Storm Boy* (Henri Safran, 1977) and *The Chant of Jimmie Blacksmith* (Fred Schepisi, 1978). Hollywood certainly provides no precedents, as its representations of children are unremittingly mawkish. From Shirley Temple to Macauley Culkin, child stars are used to play children who are precocious, cute and totally unbelievable.

In fact, British cinema, such as it is, offers many more convincing child-centred narratives than Hollywood, especially in films made during the 1960s. There may be a connection between such productions and popular nineteenth-century British fiction, for example the novels of Dickens and the Brontë sisters, in which children are frequently the focus. In any event, the child's (or children's) point of view crosses a range of genres in British cinema from drama, as in *Whistle Down the*

Wind (Bryan Forbes, 1961), to horror, as in *The Innocents* (Jack Clayton, 1961), and to comedy, as in the Launder and Gilliat St Trinian's cycle (made from 1954 to 1980).

However, the most likely inspiration for the girl-centred films that recur throughout the Australian and New Zealand women's film culture is the women's movement of the 1970s. With the foregrounding of women's experience came an interest in relationships between women (young and old) including mothers, daughters, sisters and friends, and an interest in exploring 'rites-of-passage' from childhood to adulthood from a female perspective. These subjects were often those that women short film-makers focused on (as we noted earlier) and, with time, they inevitably became a preoccupation of women feature film-makers, too.

The experiences of the child within the family are explored in the short films *A Song of Air*, *Swimming* and *A Girl's Own Story*, which all use the young female point of view (via first-person narration in *A Song of Air* and *Swimming* and through using the mechanisms of filmic identification in *A Girl's Own Story*, namely the construction of the gaze through camera and character) to expose dysfunctionality within the family context.

Feature films continue this preoccupation, ranging from the use of a young girl as protagonist in *Celia* (Ann Turner, 1988, Australia) to foregrounding the female adolescent in *My Brilliant Career* (Gillian Armstrong, 1979, Australia) and to the use of a retarded, childlike woman in *Sweetie* (Jane Campion, 1989, Australia). In these cases and many others, the world of the child (or non-adult) becomes a way of filtering or throwing into sharp relief the strangeness of a world organised and controlled by adults. Additionally, since many of these films are centrally about the female experience, the move from childhood to womanhood (with its associated 'rites-of-passage') becomes crucial. It is this experience that these films address, the first stage in a young girl's journey to independence and autonomy.

While this chapter will be concerned specifically with the devices and desires of children, it is worth noting that the child or adolescent female point of view is a feature of many other films discussed in this book. We have already seen the role of the girl in *Terra Nullius* (Ann Pratten, 1992, Australia) and in *Mauri* (Merata Mita, 1988, New Zealand) as a reference point for cultural and racial identity. The female adolescent is a feature of much of Gillian Armstrong's work, not only in *My Brilliant Career* but also in *High Tide* and *The Last Days of Chez Nous*, just as it is a feature of Jane Campion's work, too. The 'rites-of-passage' theme surfaces again in films as diverse as Monica Pellizzari's *Just Desserts* (1993, Australia), Ana Kokkinos's *Only the Brave* (1994, Australia) and Alison Maclean's *Crush* (1992, New Zealand), in which sexuality and desire conflict with mainstream values and adult repression.

The films we have chosen for discussion here all use young pre-teenage girls who are central to the film both in terms of narrative and visual articulation. It is the child's subject position that shapes the film's overall reality, and this is achieved through a number of cinematic devices which include voice-over, subjective camera shots and unexpected match shots. As such, we, the audience, are invited to see what the child (as central protagonist) sees, even though this may not be perceived by the adults around her. Thus, Celia (in the film of that title) communes quite normally with her dead granny, whom she sees on a number of occasions, just as she sees the monstrous and fantastic Hobyars, too (who are creatures out of a fairy story). In the films we have chosen to discuss, the world of the child is both more vivid than, and quite different from, the adult world in which she is placed. It is a kind of looking-glass world which has its own rituals and taboos but because it is the world legitimated by the film itself, it is the adult rituals and taboos which take on a strange and absurd aspect. With this in mind, we shall be looking at two features, *Celia* and *An Angel at My Table* (Part 1) (Jane Campion, 1990, New Zealand) and two shorts, *Rabbit on the Moon* (Monica Pellizzari, 1987, Australia, 13 mins) and *Serendipity* (Karen Borger, 1992, Australia, 17 mins).

Celia

Ann Turner's *Celia* is a complex narrative set in Australia in the late 1950s. In it, Turner uses a real-life political event (the banning of pet rabbits in Australia) to provide a metaphor for the anti-communist ethos of the day. According to Turner:

> It was about 1981 and rabbits were finally being legalised. I hadn't realised they'd been banned till then. It was such a bizarre story. I discovered that a friend of mine had to leave Melbourne in the fifties because her father was a communist and was blackbanned. The two stories fitted nicely together. Scapegoating and intolerance were the links. The government had a problem with rabbits in the country but pet rabbits weren't a part of that. It was the same with the

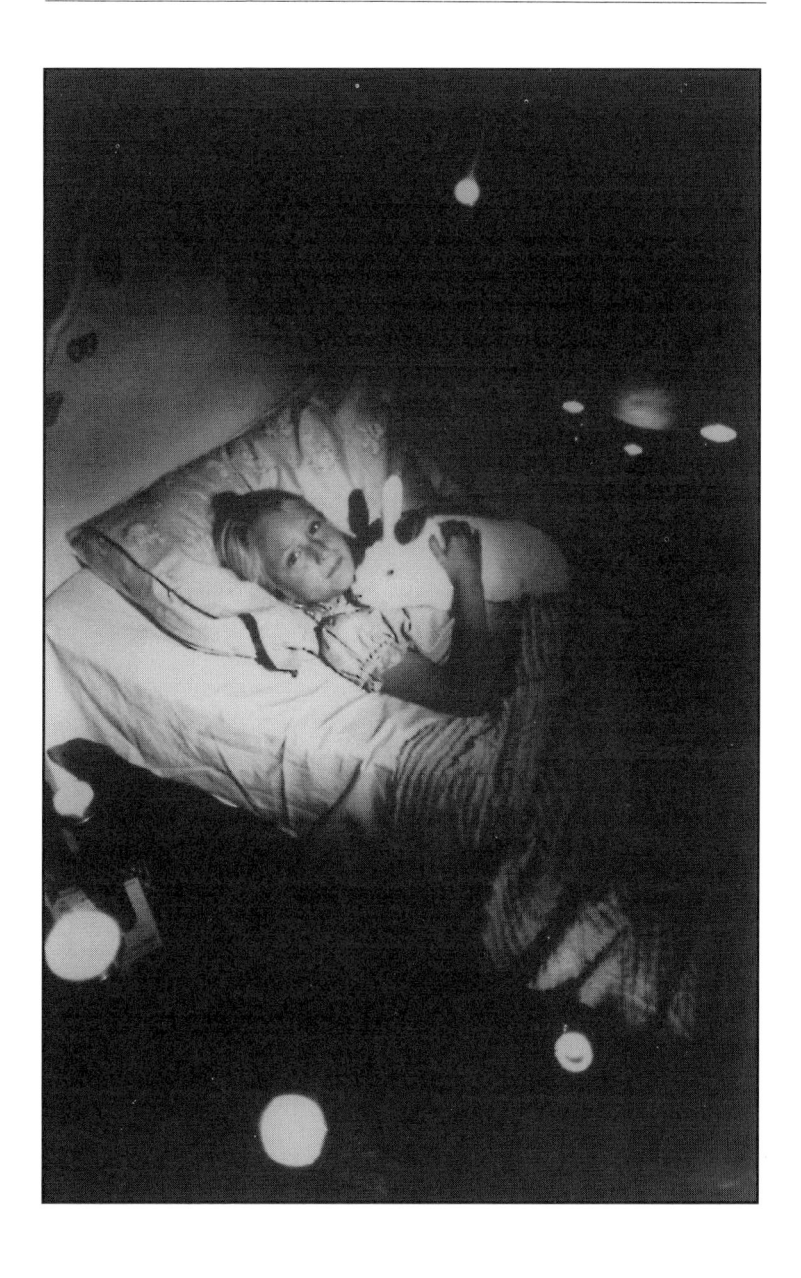

Celia (Rebecca Smart) and Murgatroyd in *Celia*
Still courtesy of BFI STILLS, POSTERS AND DESIGNS

Communist Party: the government scapegoated a group of people who weren't a threat at all.[1]

Against this backdrop, we have the story of Celia (Rebecca Smart) who is about to celebrate her ninth birthday. She is a girl with a vivid imagination and a stubborn spirit, devoted to her granny, whose death at the beginning of the film triggers off the events which follow. With the grandmother's demise, Celia's context becomes that of the standard nuclear family, comprising an authoritarian and reactionary father and a weak, conciliatory mother. Her uncle, who also lives in the suburbs, is the local policeman, a bigot whose daughter Stephanie (a spiteful goody-goody) leads the rival gang. Celia heads a gang which comprises the three Tanner children, two boys and a girl, who have just moved in next door with their parents who are communists. Celia is taken with Mrs Tanner who is enlightened and sensitive to the needs, desires and dreams of children and who is the most likeable adult in the whole story. Like Celia's granny, she is a free spirit, working for peace and socialism in contrast to the hypocrisy and small-mindedness of Melbourne suburban life.

Celia's world is one of fantasy, the cinema and gang warfare. Her parents fear the communists and she fears the Hobyars, the monstrous tribe she has heard about in the fairy stories read to her class at school. Her active imagination leads her into ritual games with her gang, involving blood pacts and moonlight sessions around a bonfire during which they exorcise their enemies (her father, Uncle Bob and Stephanie) with chants and by sticking pins in their effigies. Meanwhile, the adults in her life are engaged in their own rituals of illicit affairs, hypocrisy, accusation and counter-accusation. These two worlds converge via the cinema where the children watch public information newsreels about the plague of rabbits and thrillers about crime and murder. Using the cinema in this way, as the site in which real-life events (newsreels) and fantastic happenings (thrillers) converge, is a stroke of genius on Turner's part. As well as constructing a strong image, which conveys the mood and texture of small town, 1950s Australia, she is able to convey how, from a child's point of view, anything appearing up on the big silver screen is as authentic (or as fantastic) as anything else. Being unable to distinguish facts from fantasy is part of childhood (and in a reflexive way is also part of cinema). Adults, on the other hand, often fail to distinguish between ideology and reality (for example, Celia's mother) and some even deliberately indulge in mystification (for example, Celia's father and Uncle Bob), often to further their own interests.

A central motif of the film *Celia* is the girl's pet rabbit, Murgatroyd, who becomes a sort of touchstone against which all the characters are judged. Those who wish or do harm to Murgatroyd are bad and they include Celia's father, Uncle Bob, Stephanie and her gang and finally the state government, which brings about the rabbit's death. The film, in tune with Celia's perceptions of the world, dips in and out of realism. In this way, it avoids sentimentalising Celia, since it never shows her from the adult point of view. She is always the point of identification, being the protagonist and the character who drives the narrative forward, and in spite of experiencing injustice, even cruelty, at the hands of certain adults, she is never shown as a passive victim. Celia refuses to bend to tyranny, even when her father beats her with his belt; she stands up for what she believes in, and she finally takes her revenge against Uncle Bob, who has come to represent for her the evils of family and state alike. He is a Hobyar made flesh and Celia prepares to destroy him in a ritual where she daubs her face with rouge and lipstick. At the moment when Celia points the double-barrelled gun at Uncle Bob, we cut to a point-of-view shot and we see what she sees: an ugly, drooling Hobyar, about to pounce. She pulls the trigger and Uncle Bob falls dead at her feet.

Celia's extreme resistance to the unfair regime of adults is at first supported by Mrs Tanner and finally by her mother, who makes the decision to cover up for her daughter, even though she realises what Celia has done. The film at this point suggests a kind of female conspiracy against oppression. Certainly, it is the female characters throughout who have been the most supportive and sympathetic, from Celia's granny to Mrs Tanner and to Celia's own mother. The film ends with Celia orchestrating a mock execution to expiate Uncle Bob's murder, after which she declares that justice has been done. Our final image is of Celia as survivor, clearly in control and beginning to grasp the adult game of 'cover up'.

Rabbit on the Moon

Monica Pellizzari's *Rabbit on the Moon* is also centred round a young girl and her pet rabbit. Shot in black and white, this 13-minute short was made at AFTRS and credits Jane Campion with production advice. The child, Giuseppina, is a seven-year-old Italian-Australian, whose family from an unspecified part of Northern Italy are living in an unspecified part of Australian suburbia. Giuseppina experiences two kinds of reality: the Italian reality represented by her extended family and the Australian reality represented by school. She also constructs her own reality visually, by looking at the world through a child's telescope, so distancing herself from what is 'out there'. Sometimes she plays with her best friend who is a 'southerner' (Italian) and they light joss sticks, play the accordion, dance, and classify photographs into boxes marked 'alive', 'dead' and 'don't know'. But, in a sense, Giuseppina's fantasy life is provided by the family itself: her mysterious grandfather; her opera-singing, chicken-plucking uncle; her mother, who tells her folk stories, including one about the souls of dead rabbits which join together to form a giant rabbit on the moon. Thus, it is the vivid reality of Italian cultural life that serves as the central inspiration, both for Giuseppina and for the film itself. The film is shot often using long or middle distance to emphasise the family as characters against a rich backdrop. There is a weird and wonderful flavour about the *mise-en-scène*, as if rural Northern Italy has been transported to Australia. Composition emphasises the characters in a setting which looks as though it could be the outskirts of Florence: the porch and garden where the mother plants her corn and tomatoes; the kitchen where uncle cooks chickens and rabbits and drinks Chianti, Giuseppina's bedroom, cluttered like a bedroom in a rural cottage, stuffed full with ornaments, pots and boxes.

It is this Mediterranean expansiveness, juxtaposed with small-time suburban reality, that gives the film its surreal (almost absurd) flavour. The sound track adds to the effect. Cocks crow, chickens cluck, Italian folk music and opera are in the air. The film's rich reconstruction of Italian cultural and rural reality is enhanced by close-ups on the faces of the family, particularly the mother and the uncle, and the attention to detail is both beautiful and dramatic.

Giuseppina, like Celia, is independent, strong-willed and naughty. Like Celia, she experiences the prejudices of adult society, in her case, racism. Her father speaks of racism at work and the words 'We Love Wogs' are daubed on the garage door of their new house. At school, the children make fun of her Italian origins; she is called 'spaghetti face' and one of her schoolmates remarks that her sandwiches 'pong'.

As with the film *Celia*, the audience's identification is focused on the child and it is her point of view that predominates. Whereas Celia 'sees' things the adults cannot see, Giuseppina looks at the world differently through her telescope. At these moments, we have a subjective camera

Giuseppina (Aurelia Eneide) and her mother (Nicoletta Boris) in *Rabbit on the Moon* Still courtesy of CINENOVA shot where the image becomes a round telescopic one. We literally see the world as the child sees it. With these visual strategies, both children are shown to resist a dominant or 'acceptable' way of seeing the world. While their status within the family, school and society is one of powerlessness (both pet rabbits are killed, for example), they retreat into their own worlds of fantasy and romance and so retain a degree of autonomy and distance.

Director Monica Pellizzari has gone on to fulfil the promise she showed at AFTRS with *Rabbit on the Moon* and the short film she made a year earlier, *Velo Nero* (Black Veil). Her next short film, *Just Desserts* (1993), continues her exploration of the experiences of first- and second-generation Italian women living in Australia. Pellizzari completed her first feature film called *Fistful of Flies* in 1996 and it was screened at the London Film Festival in November of the same year. In it, Pellizzari again examines the Italian-Australian experience from the young girl's point of view and, as Lizzie Francke observes, 'astutely taps into the bizarre undercurrents of fear and loathing about female sexuality'.[2]

An Angel at My Table

An Angel at My Table (1990) was the first film Jane Campion directed in her native New Zealand. It was, in fact, made as a three-part serial for television, with funding from Television New Zealand and Channel 4, UK. It is based on the life of the New Zealand writer Janet Frame, who survived childhood poverty and eight years in mental institutions to become an acclaimed author. Made in consultation with Janet Frame, scripted by Laura Jones and starring Kerry Fox, it was released theatrically in 1991 in its three-hour epic entirety. Campion had reservations about it being shown as a film, but it became a huge international success. Part 1 of the film deals with Janet Frame's childhood and is a sensitive and moving portrayal of a shy young girl growing up in a rural family. Much softer in tone than her first Australian feature *Sweetie* (1989), Campion's comment is instructive: 'Growing up in a country as small as New Zealand, you learn a kind of respect and regard for the backward, the shy, the countrified.'[3]

In *An Angel at My Table*, the child, Janet (Alexa Keogh), is much less successful at resisting the hostile adult world than either Celia or Giuseppina. She is neither rebellious nor self-contained, but she does have a form of escape, which is through the written word. Janet loves reading and writing but, outside her books, she is extremely vulnerable

CHILD'S-EYE VIEW/**69**

Janet (Alexa Keogh) buried in a book in *An Angel at My Table*
Still courtesy of BFI STILLS, POSTERS AND DESIGNS and ARTIFICIAL EYE

and she is much more a victim than either Celia or Giuseppina. While they are all survivors, Janet is much more damaged by her experiences, as the later parts of the film show. Although, unlike Sweetie, she is not abused within the family, nevertheless the grinding poverty of their circumstances and the discrimination shown at school as a result of it cause her to withdraw into her own world. That said, the film is her story and it is told from her point of view.

Part 1 opens with her voice-over saying: 'This is the story of my childhood.' At the opening of the film, she is seven years old and the first chapter closes when she is a young woman leaving for college. The character is played by two actresses, both distinguished by shocks of unruly red hair. As a child, she is tubby and gauche. Campion's film focuses on formative moments in Janet's early life, which are experiences of suffering, at the hands of her teachers and the school authorities, and trauma, with the illness of her brother and the tragic death of her sister. Set during the depression in rural New Zealand, home life is a stark and shabby affair and Janet herself seems destined to be set apart because she is different. This difference, her naivety and sensitivity (also the basis of her talent as a writer) is represented in the film by her startling red hair. As the years pass, she becomes increasingly withdrawn and is shunned by her classmates. The relentless misery of her early years is punctuated by fleeting moments of fantasy and happiness; she reads from *The Arabian Nights*, her father gives her a notebook, the siblings create theatre in the moonlight, her English teacher recites *Morte d'Arthur*, she wins the writing prize at school.

Gradually, though, the mood of *An Angel at My Table* is one of impending despair. An early incident in the film, where she is punished by her teacher for having stolen money from her father, which she spends on sweets to distribute to her classmates, is emblematic; Janet does not understand the rules. Stylistically, Part 1 of the film is much more reminiscent of *Sweetie* than Parts 2 and 3. Camera angles and distances are unusual and unexpected, consistent with a child's perception of the world. Narratively, Part 1 has the same stark minimalism and the drama is built upon moments and incidents that are disjointed or incomplete. Overall, it constructs the sensibility of the child. The remaining two parts are much more linear and in spite of their content, which is extraordinary, they are much closer to television realism. The magical childlike quality is recaptured at the end of the film when Janet returns home, as a woman, a writer and a survivor.

Serendipity

With *Serendipity*, another short film made at AFTRS, we return to the tough, self-possessed child who creates her own world as a refuge from the adult version. This accomplished, semi-experimental drama focuses on the seven-year-old Judy whose imagination is fuelled by images from her strict Catholic upbringing. The film opens with her voice-over, as she sticks pins in dead butterflies and mounts them on lolly sticks. She places three of these into a mound of sand and calls it 'Calvary'.

Her key adult relationship is with her father, whose favourite place is his orchid house. Judy learns the Latin names of each flower and is fascinated by the plants and atmosphere in the hothouse. As she is preparing for her first communion, her father dies and we follow a subjective, shaky, hand-held Super 8 camera sequence into his bedroom where he lies. Judy's point of view is thus powerfully created. From this point on, her fascination with death, religious ritual and the orchid house grows. She becomes concerned for the souls of dead animals and collects an assortment of creatures – fish, dead frogs and a dead bird – so that she can give them a proper burial; she puts them in a shoe box and buries them in the orchid house with due ritual and ceremony. Her world of mystery is reinforced by images of the dead Jesus in church and she becomes haunted by intense visions of religious icons, flames and orchids. The film creates a mood of magic and wonder which is dreamlike and surreal. Montage sequences and Super 8 footage are used to create the effect of an innocent in a strange world. With the exception of her father and her somewhat wanton sister (a knowing adolescent), the adults are prescriptive and irritable. Her grandmother, filmed frequently from a low angle as Judy's point of view, is bossy and lacks the imagination to deal with Judy's questions about whether there are flowers in heaven, and she categorically denies that animals have souls. The priest and the other adults seem formal and insensitive and are either patronising or punitive in the way they relate to her. The film presents an adult world, the family and the church, as distant and unfeeling, lacking the rich and visual imagination of the child, who is much more in touch than they are with the emotional forces of life and death. Like Celia, she breaks the rules, steals Easter eggs from her sister and hides from her grandmother. The film, however, celebrates her disobedience as creative and life-affirming.

All the children in the films discussed in this chapter have some recourse to a world that is not available to the adults around them.

The choice, in each case, to represent the child's point of view as the most creative perspective gives the films a charm and a disarming honesty and it functions as an extremely effective critique of the repressiveness of the world of grown-ups. Celia, Giuseppina, Janet and Judy give the viewer some hope for the possibility of change, the hope that they, at least, will grow up to be different. Earlier, we argued that there were few precedents in Hollywood for films that focus on the female child or young female adolescent. It is possible, however, that this strand of film-making in Australia and New Zealand is itself influencing Hollywood, particularly in the light of the international success of films such as *An Angel at My Table* and *Celia*. In recent years, the 'rites-of-passage' film, once regarded as the exclusive domain of the young male, as least as far as Hollywood was concerned, has been shown to have a female face. Hollywood productions like *Mermaids* (Richard Benjamin, 1990), *Heathers* (Micheal Lehmann, 1989) and the more recent *Now and Then* (Lester Linka Glatter, 1995) appear to have exploited the potential that Australasian film-making has uncovered, for making movies with girls at the centre of the drama.

7

Celluloid Sisters

In Chapters 4 and 6, we noted the tendency of a number of Australasian short films (as well as features) to focus on the girl child or female adolescent, in terms of her positioning within the nuclear and (in most cases) the dysfunctional family. In this chapter, we want to look at two feature films which use another female perspective, namely the relationship between sisters, as a site for exploring the legacy of family life for women.

Sisterhood, as an irrepressible force, was a popular topic with feminists in the 1970s. The subject has strong cinematic precedents in the Hollywood melodramas of the 1940s, particularly within the sub-genre known as the 'women's picture', and here we find models for the sibling rivalry which is the focus of this chapter. In the Hollywood films, the relationship between sisters is often represented as tragically destructive, one sister (often an identical twin) having to die in order that the other can survive. To emphasise the destructive double aspect of sibling rivalry, the actress in question would play both roles, with one twin being evil (or psychotic) and the other good. This is the case, for example, with Bette Davis in *A Stolen Life* (Curtis Bernhardt, 1946) and Olivia de Havilland in *The Dark Mirror* (Robert Siodmak, 1946).[1]

Here, we will be discussing Jane Campion's first feature *Sweetie* (1989) and Gillian Armstrong's *The Last Days of Chez Nous* (1990), arguably the most innovative work by both directors to date. Although *Sweetie* was made in Australia, its references are to the New Zealand psychodrama film tradition and it has its roots not only generically but also emotionally in New Zealand soil, so to speak. It is no coincidence that, once funding was made available, Jane Campion was happy to return to her native New Zealand where she made her next two highly acclaimed films, *An Angel at My Table* (1990) and *The Piano* (1993).

A comparison between the two films reveals how much darker in mood is *Sweetie* than its more characteristically Australian sister-work, *The Last Days of Chez Nous*, even though they share many key preoccupations and are technically both Australian movies. To direct *The Last Days of Chez Nous*, Gillian Armstrong also returned home (to Australia, after working in the USA) and the film is a fine example of the Australian women's wave, a return to top form for the director. Before leaving Australia to make *Fires Within* for Pathé, Armstrong had already been approached about the *Chez Nous* project by producer Jan Chapman and had made contact with Helen Garner with whom she subsequently worked closely on the screenplay. In fact, all three women worked in close collaboration. In Armstrong's words: 'It was a very productive time, one of those situations where we were all really in tune with each other.'[2] Similarly, Jane Campion had a big involvement with the screenplay for *Sweetie*; she co-scripted it with Gerard Lee, who had been her collaborator on a number of her earlier short films.

Themes and Styles
What prompted our comparison were the remarkable thematic similarities between the two films, although stylistically they are very different. While Campion goes for a look that is precisely composed,[3] Armstrong attempts a sense of fluid transitions within the filmic space.[4] Both films have, as their structuring centre, the troubled relationship between two sisters. Both films explore how sibling relationships can threaten and even destroy other relationships, particularly with a male partner. In both films, it is the older sister's domain that is invaded by the younger. Both the younger sisters desire the stability, security and love that their siblings have seemingly found, although their respective interventions reveal that this stability is, in fact, built on shaky ground. In both films, the younger sister is needy, anarchic and egocentric, almost childlike, and in both films it is the repressed and much more responsible sister who carries the burden of guilt for herself, her sister and her family.

Within the developing drama of the sibling rivalry, both films foreground the father as a key player. It is with the father that the unease is sited; the mothers, in both films, are represented as much more practical and matter-of-fact. In both films, it is the father who provides the motivation for the trip out to the bush. In *Sweetie*, the father wants to visit his wife who has abandoned him to go and work as a cook for some jackeroos (itinerant workers on a sheep station), so the older daughter (Kay) and her boyfriend (Louis) accompany him. In *The Last Days of Chez Nous*, the father and older sister (Beth) drive into the outback as a way of redefining their relationship. In this case, Beth's partner J.P. is left behind with, as we shall see, monumental consequences. In a sense, both trips are crucial in the unfolding drama since on the return home, in both narratives, everything unravels. The respective episodes in the outback represent a strong and strange shift in the momentum of events and the films' moods. In leaving suburbia, the characters involved are thrown into another reality. The mood, the *mise-en-scène*, and the landscape are so radically different that, after the experience, nothing can be the same again. In both films, the interlude in the outback throws up a kind of return to the strange mystery that is life itself, where characters are dwarfed by their surroundings. It also serves dramatically to provide a respite from the emotional 'pressure-cooker' of suburban existence and hints at the spiritual and transformatory forces that resonate in films such as *Picnic at Hanging Rock*.

Finally, both films locate one of the key players in the drama as an outsider, outside the norm because they are different or because it is foreign to them. In *Sweetie*, it is Sweetie herself who is cast as 'other', a strange and destructive misfit who cannot be integrated into 'normal' life. In *The Last Days of Chez Nous*, it is J.P., Beth's partner, who is different, even oppositional, by virtue of his foreignness. He is French and very aware that he does not 'fit into' Australian cultural life. In both films, these 'others' become a kind of barometer for measuring the degree of dysfunctionality around them.

The formal aspects of these films are very different, but both are distinctive in ways that make them visually memorable and narratively haunting. In *Sweetie*, it is the framing, the composition and the strange colour, particularly of the interior locations, which give the film its off-beat, surreal and de-centred feel. In *The Last Days of Chez Nous*, the interiors are also striking; the use of a moving camera and close-ups highlight the strange objects and ornaments in the home itself and create a wonderful, seamless visual style and effortless pace. Both directors use musical numbers at strong emotional moments and both highlight particular motifs (food, trees, personal ornaments and objects) in extraordinarily expressive ways.

We turn now to the central relationship between the two sisters in each film in order to explore in more detail the thematic, dramatic and formal aspects of the narratives, as well as the power and beauty of both films.

Sweetie and Kay
Jane Campion's film, which on its first release ended with the dedication 'For My Sister', explores in much greater detail some of the areas touched on in her short film *A Girl's Own Story*. In that film, the point of view is that of the younger girl whose older adolescent sister is very distant. *Sweetie* replays the sibling connection (or lack of it) but the two girls are now young women. Kay (Karen Colston), the older, who is the real focus of the film, inhabits a world that is fraught with anxiety. Dawn (Genevieve Lemon), the younger sister, is also a woman but behaves like a child and is treated as such by her father who continues to address her as 'Sweetie', his pet-name for her. While Kay is almost incoherent with unexpressed rage, Sweetie prattles and preens and is clearly the embodiment of damage, as a result of her father's dubious attentions and intentions during her childhood. As such, she represents a force that is presented in the film as potentially liberational but also deeply destructive. By the end of the film, Sweetie's demise has liberated Kay and effectively destroyed the family. For the first 30 minutes of the film, the focus is entirely on Kay. Except for a brief reference to her sister who has broken the leg of one of her precious horse ornaments, a horse (as she tells the little boy next door) that she calls 'broken heart', we have no idea that Sweetie even exists. It is not until Sweetie has literally broken into her home that Kay is forced to acknowledge that she even has a sister. Even then, she initially tells Louis (her boyfriend, played by Tom Lycos) that Sweetie is a friend who is 'a bit mental'.

By now we have become aware of Kay's pathology and it is Sweetie's intervention that begins to put it into perspective. Kay is riddled with anxiety, even dread, and her approach to life is based on a deep fatalism. She is driven by superstition and a sense of fate; she got together with her boyfriend Louis entirely because a fortune-teller predicted that she would find a boy with a question mark on his forehead. Her desire is not for Louis but to keep chaos at bay and to fulfil her destiny so that by the time Sweetie arrives at the couple's home, things have already started to go wrong. Kay is scared of life, energy and sexuality. She has a phobia about trees and after a nightmare she secretly digs up and hides the sapling that Louis has planted in the back yard as a symbol of their relationship. Kay's secret serves to estrange her from Louis and she stops sleeping with him, feigning a cold. As things have gone sour between them, Kay reluctantly and unsuccessfully embarks on self-hypnosis classes, at Louis's instigation, and he, with his interest in New Age philosophy, remains by contrast quite laid-back.

Into this impasse bursts Sweetie, with a drunken no-hoper boyfriend in tow. She installs herself in the master bedroom and proceeds to have hours of unrestrained sex with the man she refers to as her 'agent'. They are both clearly going nowhere and have nowhere to go and Kay tries to get them to leave. Louis, on the other hand, is both fascinated and sympathetic. When he quizzes Kay about her sister, she replies, 'She was just born. I don't have anything to do with her.' Sweetie has told Louis that she was in a coma for a year, which is a total fabrication, and Louis describes her as 'a dark spirit'. Since Sweetie embodies everything that Kay is trying to repress, this is perceptive of him. Sweetie likes Louis and gets on well with Clayton (the small boy who lives next door), romping roughly in the garden with him. Increasingly, Kay finds herself out on a limb in this new and unwelcome set-up. Sweetie, who is obviously psychologically damaged, blithely seduces Louis on the beach by offering to lick him all over. She says: 'I'm a good licker.' Meanwhile, Kay and Louis are hardly speaking. Things move to a head when Kay once more tells Sweetie to leave. In a fit of pique, she cuts up one of Kay's dresses. Kay accuses Sweetie of treating her abusively as always, at which point Sweetie rushes into the bedroom and starts chewing up Kay's beloved horses. Kay is horrified and mortified. It appears Sweetie has not been taking her tablets.

Enter the father. This turn of events has been preceded by a short sequence, first of the exterior of the family home and a tree-house in the garden lit up with fairy lights (an important site of later action), and then of the interior, the family kitchen where the girls' mother is on the point of leaving her husband for a new life in the outback. Unable to cope, the father arrives at Kay's front door with a stack of frozen dinners, labelled with days of the week. Kay, who has obviously taken pains to get away from her family members, now finds herself besieged by them.

Sweetie, in anarcho-punk regalia, black nail varnish, black fishnet stockings, is seen talking in a seemingly reasonable fashion to her father about show business. Kay, displaced and increasingly de-centred (in narrative terms as well as by the camera angles and frame composition), tries to protest. Her father says sorrowfully: 'I thought I brought you two kids up to love each other.' The extremity of this delusion is echoed in his approach to Sweetie. He seems to defer to her decision to make it: 'The show world is full of unusual types,' he says. He is clearly responsible for Sweetie's state and colludes with her fantasies. As if to underline this, the film cuts to a flashback motivated by his memory of Sweetie as a gauche young girl, bespectacled and unprepossessing, in a tutu doing a ballet routine, diving into her father's arms in a graceless and somewhat precocious manner. We cut back to the present and an overweight, deluded and out of control adult, whose father's unwavering question, 'Has she got a chance?' goes unanswered. She is still 'Dad's real girl' and his 'princess' but he is as lost as she is in self-delusion and denial. Kay has to face her exclusion from their 'special relationship' and also her own collusion with the family's silence around it. We see her catch sight of Sweetie sponging down her father's body and we see her moment of recognition, the realisation of the family's dirty secret to which she has been privy and of which she is part.

At this point we reach the film's final movement. Kay, Louis and the father leave for the outback to visit the mother and they conspire to leave Sweetie behind. It is the father who finally dupes Sweetie into leaving the car in which she has installed herself, and as they depart in getaway mode, he is thrown into despair. During what can only be described as a surrealist interlude at the jackeroos' camp, which is more high camp than light relief but certainly a magical and strangely peaceful period, the family together decide that Sweetie must be dealt with. The mother is matter-of-fact, almost fatalistically resigned. She says of her husband: 'He's in a fix about her. He's under her thumb. He's scared stiff.'

Their return home marks the final unravelling. Sweetie, in a now chaotic house, surrounded by disorder and wreckage, has descended into a catatonic rage. She pulls her sweater over her head and growls menacingly in response to her father's greeting of 'Hello, little puppy!' Mayhem ensues; the parents leave with Sweetie, Louis leaves Kay who, now that she is alone, becomes almost completely dysfunctional, sleeping on the front lawn and unable to cope. Meanwhile, back at the family home, things have gone from bad to worse. Sweetie has installed herself in the tree-house and refuses to come down. She has stripped naked and daubed herself with paint and leaves. Kay is summoned and arrives with Clayton, in the hope that he can help to lure his friend Sweetie from the tree. As it turns out, he gleefully joins

Dawn (Genevieve Lemon) dressing up in *Sweetie*
Still courtesy of BFI STILLS, POSTERS AND DESIGNS and ELECTRIC PICTURES

Sweetie in the tree-house in a childish escapade, and together they whoop and fart in the face of the adults. The father, defeated, lies alone on Sweetie's bed, while Kay and her mother call the fire brigade. But events are now beyond rescue. Sweetie, jumping up and down manically, splits the wooden floor of the tree-house and plunges through it to her death. Kay tries to save her with the kiss of life (the first physical contact we have seen between them) but it is too late. At the funeral, a root from a nearby tree has to be sawn off before the coffin can be lowered; before its descent, Kay touches the coffin in a farewell gesture. Now her nails are painted black, just as her sister's used to be. This is a measure of Kay's shift and her liberation. She has already begun a tentative repair of her relationship with Louis; we cut to a shot of her horse ornaments, damaged but now lovingly repaired with glue and sticky tape. Her father's farewell is less promising: 'Goodbye, Sweetie, good girl.'

The final sequence of the film is motivated by the father's memory. Its effect is strange and surreal. Sweetie, as an apparition, almost like a vision of a child-saint, stands plaintively singing 'With Every Beat of My Heart', almost as if she is rehearsing for a talent contest, miming each phrase, in a mawkish and over-sentimentalised routine. The entire image is deeply unsettling; Dad's 'real girl' returns to her father, like the repressed, from beyond the grave.

As for the two sisters, Kay, as indicated, is on a course of mending and there is a sense at least in which Sweetie has had to be sacrificed for this to be possible. Jane Campion comments on this in an interview:

> [I]n *Sweetie* Kay comes to a big realisation. I wanted to show that, of all the family, Kay knew what went on with Sweetie. But she's also angry with her. At the end, she's the only one able to act to try and save her sister, give her mouth to mouth, which is very intimate. There was a definite 'Live! you don't have to die for me to exist.' I think sometimes Kay thought it would be impossible to be herself and live and have a love affair with Louis without Sweetie being absent or dead.[5]

Vicki and Beth

As we have already noted, *The Last Days of Chez Nous* provides an interesting comparison with *Sweetie*. Generically and stylistically too, Armstrong's film is much less of a psychodrama and much more a melodrama, realist rather than surrealist. As Cairo Cannon says of *The*

Last Days of Chez Nous: '[it] deals with themes of home, family, relationships and food: themes perceived as traditional women's territory'.[6] The characters in *The Last Days of Chez Nous* are more rounded, more conventionally realised than those in *Sweetie*. This is not a criticism of Campion's film, where the characterisation is deliberately off-kilter, de-centred both psychologically and compositionally. Similarly, Campion's style is sparse, creating a mood that is edgy and unsettling. *The Last Days of Chez Nous*, by contrast, is mellow, the atmosphere created is almost nostalgic, suffused with a sense of regret at the impending loss. Settings and camera movements amplify this contrast. Campion's suburbia is represented in shallow space and the frame compositions are deliberately asymmetric. The house where Kay lives, however, is presented with a long linear track down a uniform street, emptied almost of all life and detail. *Chez Nous* by contrast is depicted in terms of depth of field. We move forward into the house from a long shot of a leafy, affluent suburb in Sydney, moving gradually into close-up through the window of the house. The effect of this is to bring the audience close to the dramatic focus of the film, whereas in *Sweetie* the effect is to distance us.

The narrative of *The Last Days of Chez Nous*, which like *Sweetie* is episodic in form, highlighting key moments of development, begins with the arrival of Vicki (Kerry Fox), Beth's younger sister, from her travels in Europe. Beth (Lisa Harrow) has baked a heart-shaped welcome-home cake, and Vicki's first action is to carve out a huge wedge which she casually, almost cruelly, crams into her mouth. It is a gesture which, as Lizzie Francke observes, 'is symbolic of her greedy desire, a hunger that makes her careless of others'.[7] Vicki throws up almost immediately afterwards. We learn later that she is pregnant.

Superficially at least, the relationship between the two sisters in *The Last Days of Chez Nous* appears to be much fonder than that between Sweetie and Kay. Closer inspection and telling moments, however, reveal Chez Nous as a simmering site of tension, frustrations and rivalry, not only between the sisters, Beth and Vicki, but also between Beth and her partner, J.P. (Bruno Ganz). The relationships in the film, which are its central concern, can be represented as a series of shifting triangles in which, at any particular moment, one of the three central characters, Beth, Vicki or J.P., feels excluded or betrayed by the other two. As Raffaele Caputo has remarked:

[T]he central focus of the film resides with how interpersonal relationships develop and change and get chiselled out of a peculiar environment or setting. Armstrong has succeeded in shaping for *The Last Days of Chez Nous* an odd, complicated balance of symmetrical and unsymmetrical actions and events.[8]

These structuring patterns, represented below in diagrammatic form, allow the film to express a range of differing and often conflicting points of view at various moments:

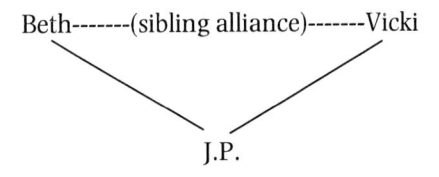

```
Beth-------(sibling alliance)-------Vicki
         \                       /
          \                     /
           \                   /
                 J.P.
```

Figure 1. The situation as seen from J.P.'s point of view: a feeling of betrayal and exclusion by the sisters.

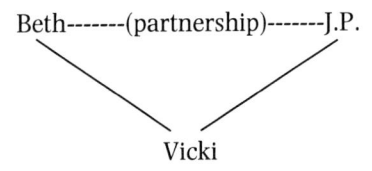

```
Beth-------(partnership)-------J.P.
         \                   /
          \                 /
           \               /
               Vicki
```

Figure 2. The situation as seen from Vicki's point of view: a feeling of envy for her sister's relationship.

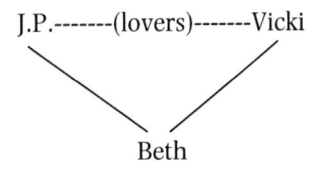

```
J.P.-------(lovers)-------Vicki
       \               /
        \             /
         \           /
             Beth
```

Figure 3. The situation as seen from Beth's point of view: a feeling of betrayal by husband and sister.

The effect of the complex relationships between the major players, and the shifting focus of the film from one to another, allow the audience to identify with all of them, so that, although Beth clearly emerges as the film's ultimate focus, she (like Vicki and J.P.) is shown as relatively sympathetic as well as being at the same time insensitive to the needs of the others. This expansiveness of approach to the characters is a rare achievement and is a measure of the strength and sensitivity of both the screenplay and Armstrong's direction.

It is interesting to note that the other two characters within the household, Annie (Miranda Otto), Beth's teenage daughter, and Tim (Kiri Paramore), a young student lodger, are not locked into the competing patterns just described. Their developing closeness and easy harmony can be seen as an example of what is possible, a kind of idealised version of what a relationship can be. It is something of what Beth aspires to, both with J.P., her husband, and also her father, but is unable to achieve completely, despite some kind of resolution at the end of the film.

As for the two sisters, Vicki's dependence on Beth is established early. Her almost childish demands and naive approach to the real world make her at the same time irritating and endearing. She is not damaged like Dawn in *Sweetie* but she is spoilt and indulged by her older sister whom she has opted to regard as a parent, judging her real parents 'too old' to understand her. While expecting to be mothered, protected and defended by Beth, Vicki also aspires to be what Beth is, a successful writer, and have what Beth has, a successful relationship. She has, however, no real sense of having to work to achieve these goals. When she quizzes Beth on how to become a writer, she is petulant at Beth's response: Beth says, 'Why don't you just start?', and Vicki retorts, 'It's all right for you!' The fact that she is unwilling to put herself out is observed by both J.P. and Annie who see her as an indolent spectator when household chores need doing. Annie who is the real daughter and the real child is ironically much more independent and self-motivated. J.P. is appalled by Vicki's laziness and shallowness, commenting that she should read some real news, as she leafs idly through a gossipy magazine.

At the same time as criticising Vicki's indolence, J.P. is clearly attracted to her youthful and anarchic energy when she is playing (dancing, singing, dressing up) and he joins in with her revelling in the exuberance she brings to the home. Meanwhile, Beth defends Vicki from criticism, humours her chaotic impulses and seems happy to play Martha to Vicki's Mary. She cooks, cleans, tidies up and generally organises the other members of the household in a benign but controlling way. Chez Nous is a symbol of her endeavours, a labour of love, kept together by her need to have things in their right place both aesthetically and emotionally.

Just as Dawn's arrival exposes the problems between Kay and Louis, Vicki's arrival is a catalyst to things falling apart between Beth and J.P. Their relationship is not the bed of roses Vicki imagines. J.P. is frustrated in his marriage and feels out on a limb with the sisters' easy allegiance. As a Frenchman, he feels marginalised both within Chez Nous and within Australia as a whole. He responds to Beth's orderliness with Gallic contempt and feels hurt and frequently humiliated by her treatment of him. His masculinity is threatened by Beth's brusque feminism and their relationship has increasingly become a charade. Beth, despite being both a mother and successful writer, is herself deeply disturbed by J.P.'s obvious sexual rejection of her. She fills the growing gulf between them with mindless chatter or recriminations. They are at breaking point but Beth refuses to acknowledge it. Instead, she embarks on a trip with her father to work on her relationship with him, in spite of the fact that the relationship at home is much more pressing. As Armstrong remarked in an interview, by going on a trip Beth gains a father but loses a husband.[9]

In the film, Armstrong seems to be testing the feminist values that underpin Beth's existence. Beth's beliefs are shown throughout the film to be formulaic, rigid precepts by which she orders and gives meaning to her life. Her assumptions about Vicki's pregnancy prove to be a major stumbling block. She persuades her sister to get an abortion and fails to notice Vicki's unhappiness. 'You made the right decision, Vicki. I'm absolutely sure you did.' In standing by 'a woman's right to choose', Beth has ironically denied Vicki any real choice in the matter. Like Kay in *Sweetie*, Beth, being the much more responsible sister, is also the more repressed, staying firmly in denial as the torrent rages around her. In the end, her desire to control the lives of the two people she loves the most drives them into one another's arms.

During her expedition with her father, things at Chez Nous unravel. It is as though Beth's absence has liberated the remaining members of the household who embark upon relationships that, if there, Beth would not have countenanced. Tim and Annie begin a sweet romance, J.P. and Vicki an adulterous passion. The place becomes a mess; no one seems to care or even notice. On hearing of Beth's return, J.P. says, 'We haven't cleaned up,' to which Vicki replies, 'It's too late now. Love is more important than housework.'

Beth returns to face the music: her daughter and the lodger at the piano, totally absorbed in each other; Chez Nous in total disarray; her husband declaring his love for her sister. Significantly, on hearing this devastating news, Beth locks herself into a room and proceeds to smash all the china ornaments and articles that she has so lovingly and painstakingly assembled over the years of her life at Chez Nous. This focus on the emotional importance of objects recalls Kay's affection for her china horses, motifs representing the memory of love and security.

The final movement of the film suggests the calm after the storm. There is a sense that Beth and J.P. can rebuild a relationship as close friends but Beth's damaged relationship with Vicki is not available for repair in the same way. When they meet, Vicki refuses to acknowledge the depth of her betrayal of Beth. She says almost sulkily, 'Love's more important than anything', and in a moment of clarity, Beth severs the ties of co-dependency that have bound them together. 'I can't do anything to help you anymore,' she says.

Just as in *Sweetie*, we are left with the feeling that the bond between sisters, forged as it is within the family, can be so destructive that only death (or, as in the case of Beth and Vicki, estrangement) can allow at least one sister to flourish. There is a sense in which Beth can now become a good and real mother to Annie whose needs were hitherto overshadowed by the demands of Vicki, the pretend daughter. As with Kay in *Sweetie*, the final moments of the film suggest Beth rising from the ashes of a devastated dependency and damaged domesticity. The younger sister, in both *Sweetie* and *The Last Days of Chez Nous*, has been a catalyst to chaos, blowing apart a repressive edifice constructed by the older one. An adage from the women's movement seems apt: Sisterhood is powerful – it kills, sisters!

8

Disrupting the Family

We turn now to focus on the role of the female outsider, the woman as predator, as she is represented in two Australasian films of very different moods. *Crush* was directed in New Zealand by Alison Maclean in 1992 and bears many of the hallmarks of the New Zealand psychodrama. Despite some moments of irony and unsettling humour, the film's overall mood is dark, contrasting vividly with the mood and style of the second film we shall be considering here, *Dallas Doll*, made by Australian director Ann Turner in 1994. This film also features a destructive female protagonist (who, like her sister in *Crush*, is an American with dubious morals) but the mood is now clearly comic and satirical.

Crush
Crush was Alison Maclean's first feature film. It was an official entry for Cannes in 1992 and was shown at the London Film Festival in 1993. It was produced by Bridget Ikin for Hibiscus Films, in association with the New Zealand Film Commission. Ikin had produced Campion's film *An Angel at My Table* two years earlier and, in 1989, Maclean's disturbing short film *Kitchen Sink*, which is discussed elsewhere. Some of this film's preoccupations (with the monstrous and with body horror) are picked up again in *Crush* so that just as Campion's short film *A Girl's Own Story* is almost a dress rehearsal for *Sweetie*, so *Kitchen Sink* is, in some ways, a rehearsal for *Crush*.

At the centre of the narrative is a friendship between two women, the New Zealand journalist Christina (Donogh Rees), and her anarchic American friend Lane (Marcia Gay Harden). When Lane crashes the car they are travelling in, Christina is badly hurt and hospitalised; Lane continues the journey to Rotorua and decides to keep Christina's appointment with the writer Colin (William Zappa). Colin lives with his fifteen-year-old daughter Angela (Caitlin Bossley), and both are vulnerable and easy prey for Lane. Meanwhile, Christina emerges slowly from her coma in hospital, encouraged by Angela who takes an interest in her and who is spurred on by jealousy and anger at her father's obsessive relationship with Lane. Angela secretly arranges for Christina, now in a wheelchair and seriously brain-damaged, to join them all by the lake. The next day, when the four of them are out walking in the bush, Christina pushes Lane to her death from a high look-out platform.

Identities
Though billed in some quarters as a tale of seduction and revenge, the film's key preoccupation is with identity and role, with belonging and recognition (and their opposites). In the opening sequences, Lane is clearly established as needy, childlike and intrusive, as she greedily accepts food from Christina and eats it noisily, in close-up, with cheeks bulging and her full red mouth moist. In the car, she seizes Christina's notebook and in the badinage that follows, there is a clear suggestion that these two women may be lovers. Lane, the out-of-control, prying child, represents excess and sensuality; Christina, the adult or mother figure, is intellect and rationality – but the car crash changes everything.

As Lane staggers from the wreckage, she picks up her scattered belongings and then checks her face in the car's wing mirror, as if to reassure herself of her survival and her identity. Later, she tells Angela, 'I thought you were a boy', and Angela, for her part, initially assumes Lane is Christina. Christina herself, since the accident, is unrecognisable.

Mirrors, reflections and photographs are used to facilitate key recognitions (often with sexual overtones) and shifts in perception. Lane lends Angela a red dress, in a deliberate attempt to feminise her and make her less 'non-commercial' as she puts it. In this film, the colour red symbolises desire and as they face the mirror side by side, Angela holding the red dress in front of her, Lane converts false eyelashes into a moustache; they are man and woman, momentarily; we cut to Angela, now wearing the red dress at home and dancing in front of her own mirror; on the sound track, we hear the words of a song: 'it's a dangerous game'.

Later, in a sequence which is strongly reminiscent of *Kitchen Sink*, Lane cuts Colin's hair and holds up the shiny toaster for him to check

'I thought you were a boy': Lane (Marcia Gay Harden) and Angela (Caitlin Bossley) in *Crush*
Still courtesy of BFI STILLS, POSTERS AND DESIGNS and METRO TARTAN

his reflection; as they kiss, over his shoulder the scissors are wide open in her hand. Later still, when Angela is burning with rejection ('You're sore at me 'cos your best friend turned out to be a father-fucker,' Lane says), she cuts Lane's head out of a photograph and shows it to Christina in the hospital, in an effort to engender recognition and hostility: 'This is the person that did this to you,' says Angela.

Family roles and sexual identities shift throughout the narrative. Into the family with no mother comes Lane (with her strange, ungendered name) to seduce the father and the daughter, prepared at moments to play the mother, at other times to be the wayward, hostile and intensely vulnerable child. Angela, the daughter, and not yet lover, becomes mother to Christina, now in a damaged and regressed childlike state. Colin, the father, clumsy and desperate for physical love, is uneasy with his daughter's emerging maturity. Helpless and obsessed, he is reduced to violence and despair by his desire for Lane.

Against this dysfunctional, would-be family are set the values of the indigenous Maori community. In the hospital, as Angela looks on at the helpless Christina, the Pakeha doctor describes his comatose patient as being like a still lake, 'all that life teeming beneath the surface'. Referring to Maori spiritual beliefs, he says, 'We have a lot to learn from the tangata whenua' ('people of the land'). What Christina needs, he says, is spiritual sustenance; 'that's where the family comes in, the whanau'. The Maori family is typically an extended one, as we saw in our discussion of the film *Mauri*. Shortly afterwards, still in the hospital and drawn by the sound of laughing and talking, Angela is briefly welcomed into just such a community, a gathering of Maori around the bedside of Horse, the night-club singer (played by Pete Smith). The shared sense of ease and belonging, the nurturing, the jokes, the expansive gestures provide a striking contrast with Angela's own 'family' and with Christina's isolation and suffering, just a few yards away.

Intrusions
Just as Pakeha have intruded into Maori culture, so too, the film suggests, America has intruded into New Zealand and corrupted its lifestyle and values. Lane personifies this intrusion; moments before they crash, Christina is telling her that the landscape has no predators, that it is 'totally benign', a kind of 'prelapsarian world'; it has been described as a landscape for too few lovers, she says: 'But you'll fix that, won't you, Lane?'

Just as Lane wreaks havoc in the lives of others, so she is a misfit in the landscape and the culture. When she stumbles out of the wrecked car in which Christina remains trapped, she teeters about in heeled boots on the grassy slope and, later, under Angela's disapproving gaze, she slips and slides on the grey volcanic mud, in ungainly and inappropriate dress. She is dismissive of Maori customs ('The less I know about a place, the more I like it') and refuses to share Angela's pride in the scenery ('What do you do around here for entertainment?').

In her ignorance and brashness, she is, in fact, the embodiment of the American tourist as typically perceived in New Zealand; the smaller, less secure country has borrowed much from America and, as Maclean notes in an interview, has the deepest scorn for its values. But this is the other 'crush', the hopelessly imbalanced flirtation which, like Angela's attachment to Lane, can only end in disaster. Americans have power but lack sincerity; like the huge cardboard mannequin of the woman at the roadside (which we glimpse briefly before the car crash and which distracts Lane's attention so disastrously), like the mannequin of the Maori maiden outside the tourist shop in the township, they do not fit with the land. Near the end of the film, at the lakeside, with the battle lines between Angela and Lane firmly drawn, they discuss America's cultural and economic power; 'America's history', says Angela. Indeed, the ending of the film, in which Lane perches precariously, in her final act of foolishness, before plunging to her death at Christina's hand, did apparently cause some offence to Americans and was intended in some ways, Maclean says, to represent the revenge of New Zealand on America.[1]

A primal landscape
The film's main location is Rotorua, a sacred Maori site also renowned for the intensity of its geothermal activity. The opening shot of the film, over which the titles are played, is a close-up of a seething, spurting mass of orange, boiling mud, an emblem of the emotional turbulence to come. Maori mythology draws on the mystery and energy of this landscape and some see it as a metaphor for the origins of life itself. It is unstable and unpredictable, likely to erupt at any time, impossible to control.

At moments of emotional intensity, the film cuts abruptly to this turbulent landscape. Following the fight with her father, Angela retreats outdoors; against leaden 'out of season' skies, the steam rises around her. From Horse's groans of pleasure as Angela stimulates him, we cut to the steam rising from the hot pool she has immersed herself in. From the violence of Christina's outburst when, in her wheelchair, she charges into the room at night and disrupts Colin's and Lane's lovemaking, we cut immediately to a close-up of the seething and turbulent wake of a launch. Finally, it is this mysterious, unpredictable landscape which swallows up Lane, the predator, who disappears without trace into the roaring water at the bottom of the ravine. When she has gone, the camera tilts up, to the mountains and green forests which stretch into the distance as far as the eye can see, before the image fades, giving place to the final titles. The landscape works in this film as the music does, to underscore the emotional crises and to put the characters' actions into a wider, cosmic perspective.

'Off-kilter horror'
Crush might be described as 'melodramatic' in such things as its use of the landscape and music at moments of heightened emotion and in its concern with relationships and the family, albeit a fragmented one. But it has, too, links with both the horror film and the *film noir* genres.

As noted above, Maclean's earlier short, *Kitchen Sink*, dealt with aspects of the monstrous and here, too, this concern is evident. Despite her vulnerability, Lane has 'monstrous' characteristics; not only does she leave her seriously injured friend at the roadside but she can 'turn' quickly and, at one point, she arrives back at the house to find Angela with Christina's notebook. She is shown framed by the doorway, clad in black, hooded in a motorbike helmet, a sinister figure in an uncontrollable rage, a low growling noise on the sound track. In an effort to retrieve the notebook, she violently attacks first Angela and then Colin.

In some senses, she is the classic 'femme fatale' from the *film noir*, with seductive ways, enough vulnerability to convince, and a selfish, exploitative outlook. She is a clear threat to the established order and, like many femmes fatales before her, at the end, she is physically eliminated. Compared to the female protagonists in the anti-feminist films produced by Hollywood in the late 1980s and early 1990s, however, such as *Fatal Attraction* (Adrian Lyne, 1987), *Single White Female* (Barbet Schroeder, 1992) or *The Hand That Rocks the Cradle* (Curtis Hanson, 1992), Lane and Dallas (as we see below) are both far less demonised and much less depraved. These Australasian female protagonists do intrude and they do disrupt the patriarchal family, chiefly through their sexual ambiguity and opportunism. But here the family is itself problematised and represented as ripe for destruction; it is far from sacred and has none of the idealised qualities of the Gallagher family in *Fatal Attraction*, for example. Lane and Dallas (in *Dallas Doll*) both act as catalysts, splitting open family structures that are shown to be already fatally flawed.

Crush is also concerned with horror, particularly body horror, and in sequences such as the hair-cutting described above, or when an angry Angela swirls long dark hairs in the bath tub, there are sinister references to *Kitchen Sink*. But the real horror in this film is the deformed and disabled Christina. In the hospital, she performs the acts of a lunatic, wildly throwing food around, baring her breast gleefully, and defecating over the doctor's shoes. When the reconciliation with Lane comes, such as it is, and they hug, the camera focuses on Christina's swollen, disfigured face and, from behind Lane's shoulder, we see Christina's eyes roll ghoulishly. There is menace in her look; this 'monster' seeks revenge.

Maclean's interest in the darker side of female friendships and in the complexity of human motivations comes across strongly in this film. In some important ways, her female characters remain unknowable: 'I am interested in films where there's a character that's slightly archetypal, or unreal and real at the same time, never fully fleshed out.'[2]

In addition, as Lizzie Francke notes, this 'off-kilter horror' film is 'conspicuously uncosy about female friendships'[3] and in its off-beat, unsettling way, it has clear links with films by other Australasian women.

Dallas Doll

One such film is *Dallas Doll* (1994) directed by Ann Turner, whose first feature film *Celia* is discussed elsewhere. Developed with the assistance of the Australian Film Commission and made with the participation of the Australian Film Finance Corporation, as well as the Australian Broadcasting Commission and the BBC, *Dallas Doll* stars American actress and comedian Sandra Bernhard (as Dallas) and Victoria Longley (as Rosalind). Bernhard's cult figure status (at one time, she was reported as having a lesbian relationship with Madonna) and her sexual ambiguity are fully exploited in the film which was shown at the London Film Festival in 1994. On the surface, there is little to connect this film with *Celia*, though Victoria Longley appears in both and both films do, in their different ways, offer serious critiques of Australian suburban mores and lifestyles.

Role plays
Dallas Adair is an American golfing guru. Her novel teaching technique involves the use of 'group therapy', accompanied by much baring of the soul (and some other things besides) and a lot of psycho-babble. She descends on the Sommers family home in Sydney like a storm and proceeds to wow them all (all, that is, except daughter Rastus, played by Rose Byrne, and the family dog, Argus). Her sexual ambiguity is heavily signposted on her arrival at the house (for a 'just delicious' meal of fried wombat) by a prolonged close-up of her trousered legs and manly shoes, descending from the car and approaching the gate. She seduces, in turn, the teenage son Charlie (Jack Blundell), husband Stephen (Frank Gallacher), and Charlie's mom, Rosalind, all of whom are portrayed as lost suburban souls, searching for meaning in their empty lives.

Charlie meets Dallas on the plane back from America to Australia; he is enamoured with America and warns Dallas that Australia's 'not as good as America'. Charlie is convinced that fate has brought Dallas to the Sommers home. Rosalind is also needy and dreams of devouring confectionery castles in fields of sunflowers. Stephen, it turns out, needs pain and enjoys a bit of sadism. Rastus is also seeking answers but she is not fooled by Dallas and looks instead to the stars and the cosmos; while other members of her family are busily weaving a web of adultery and betrayal, Rastus goes on searching the skies for signs of UFOs, her monosyllabic boyfriend Eddy at her side. 'You're a sucker, Rastus,' says her brother, but then so it seems is he, and when a sceptical Dallas confronts Rastus one evening, Rastus replies, 'Yeah, well, even if it is bullshit at least it's *my* bullshit; I'd rather swallow that than your crap.'

In this film, suburbia is an accident waiting to happen. Rastus apart, Dallas's 'crap' falls on fertile ground. As she says when Rosalind invites her to stay: 'I enjoy staying with families. I've been put up by a lot of them. Who knows? We could have fun.'

Encounters with aliens
Dallas (as her name suggests) is a personification of America, as perceived by Australia. As we noted above in connection with *Crush*, Australasian perceptions of the USA are characterised by notions of

exploitation (moral, intellectual, financial and political) and like Lane, Dallas is 'larger than life', an alien and disruptive force – but this time played for laughs. 'Ooooo . . . 'says Rastus in disgust, when Charlie confesses to having had sex with Dallas. 'Think of where she's been, . . . all those American germs!'

Dallas will go to any lengths to get what she wants. The money for 'Doll Links', a golf course 'for the children', comes from some Japanese businessmen who stand, bemused, at the opening ceremony (and are even more bemused by the 'group therapy' sessions which follow and which are translated in all their revealing detail). In the 1990s context of an influx of Asian business interests into Australia, Turner pushes the satire home; moments after Dallas's speech of welcome ('Give me the child until he's seven and I will give you the golfer'), a Japanese businessman cracks open a bottle of champagne on a doll's head.

This is a land where everyone can have what they want. 'You believe in fate, Charlie,' says Dallas, 'I believe in opportunity.' The script is full of sound-bites and Charlie and Stephen both start to talk like the alien Dallas. When Rosalind confesses to Stephen that she has fallen in love with Dallas, he says he already knows: 'Oh, Ros, you're so conservative, you've got to learn to move with the times . . . *l'air du temps* . . . this beats the nuclear family hands down. We'll all be happy!' And then as Rosalind flees in panic, he calls after her, 'You can lose us both or you can have us all!'

Ironically, it is the other 'alien presences' in the film that finally see off Dallas. She cannot (for all her claims to the contrary) communicate with animals at all and Argus, the dog, hostile towards her from her arrival, has never forgiven her for hitting him on the head with a golf ball. In a sequence that Francke suggests may be the first in a fiction film to feature a dog's nightmare,[4] he dreams of tearing apart a stuffed doll and, in the bizarre final movement of the film, when Dallas has fallen down a UFO crater, it is Argus who races to release the stampede of cattle, so bringing about her demise. Just as animals are hostile towards her, so the paranormal is not within her ken either and as she lies helpless she is dazzled by the bright lights of the UFO. Some forces are, finally, beyond her control.

Anarchy in the suburbs
The effect of Dallas's weird invasion into the ordered world of suburbia is ultimately to parody that world itself in all its manifestations. The film is stuffed full of icons of middle-class suburbia: gardens, dolls, pets,

mini-golf. And nothing is as it should be; the garden hose can curl like a serpent, the dolls are subject to abuse, the animals have attitude problems and mini-golf becomes a game of strip-poker. As Dallas and Rosalind prance round the indoor mini-golf circuit in their underwear, clutching glasses of 'bubbly' and shooting miniature golf balls up the trunks of miniature elephants, the sound track provides a delightful irony. The song 'A Woman's Touch' (from the Hollywood film *Calamity Jane*) now has clear sexual overtones as Dallas leads Rosalind into the bedroom.

The activities of the middle classes outside their homes are not immune from criticism either. The local town hall politicians are figures of fun and those searching for 'deeper meanings' are mocked, too. When Charlie finds Dallas in his father's bed and runs away, he heads for the outback; he asks a group of Aboriginals by the roadside whether the circling birds are an omen. 'You'll believe anything!' they say, laughing at him. Charlie's preoccupation with the meaning of a pair of cuff-links and even, finally, Rastus's desire to spot a UFO are curious New Age diversions; for the gullible, symbols are everywhere.

The film defies easy classification. Some of the sequences have a surreal quality (as in the opening, for example, where Charlie dreams he finds the cuff-link, or shortly afterwards when Dallas has been attacked by Argus, and the garden hose comes to life). At other times, and especially at the end, it resembles a parody of a 'close encounters' movie. The humour is delightfully droll throughout. The movie is, in fact, an anarchic romp through a whole range of styles, a parody even of comedy itself.

Its real achievement, however, is to be both funny *and* political, and in the context of this book it stands out from other work by Australian and New Zealand women for this reason. In the final sequences of the film, with Dallas gone (though preserved for ever in statue form – 'Like Our Lord Jesus Christ, she was a fisher of men . . . and women,' says the vicar), Rosalind is on her own. Stephen has taken to inflicting himself with cigarette burns, Charlie is a cool, self-made man. Rosalind has the farm of her dreams and now she distances herself from both of them: 'I lived for a long time letting people carve out chunks of me, thinking that was best for everyone,' she says to Charlie. 'I was too frightened to think of who I was. I'll be here for you – but I'm not selling.' Rastus and boyfriend Eddy are throwing bales of hay to the cattle as Rosalind climbs into the tractor and heads off to the top field; Charlie watches as she recedes into the golden landscape, a small figure in the bottom corner of the frame; we cut to a close-up of Charlie and then the camera moves down to his shirt sleeves where he is fingering Dallas's cuff-links. There is a brief shot of Argus, also looking after Rosalind, and then a cut to Rosalind riding towards the camera through the golden sunflowers filling the frame, the wind blowing her hair, smiling broadly. 'I'm awake and I jump for joy, I'm on my own,' goes the song on the sound track. Rosalind has extricated herself, she is a woman empowered. Though the family has been disrupted and will never be the same again, Rosalind is strong, at peace with herself and the land.

9
Women Displaced

Both of the films we consider here were made by women directors returning home to their native countries after periods of successful filmmaking elsewhere. In connection with the making of *High Tide* (1987), Gillian Armstrong, who had just completed *Mrs Soffel* for MGM in Hollywood, comments on the pleasures of creative independence and of having financial control again.[1] Jane Campion, too, has spoken of the joy she felt in returning to New Zealand from Australia to film. Interestingly, both *High Tide* and *The Piano* centre specifically on women who are themselves displaced and estranged in different ways and who make journeys that bring them face to face with neglected aspects of their lives.

In both films, landscape is used effectively as a backdrop to the women's struggles and to emphasise the precariousness of their marginal positions. The sweeping coastline and beaches of *High Tide* and the thick mud and dense impenetrable undergrowth of *The Piano* are filmed in ways that are reminiscent of *Trial Run* where landscape takes on a visceral quality, has a life of its own and becomes almost a character in the drama.

Another key similarity between the two films that we discuss here is their concern with performance and masquerade, with deception and concealment through dressing up and disguise. Both female protagonists use dress and costume, in deliberate and knowing ways, to conceal and defuse their real power and the threat which they pose to an established regime. In *High Tide*, Lilli's performance (as dancer and stripper) is her defence against the real world as well as her means of survival within it. Ada, in *The Piano*, barters with her Victorian costume. This begins as a survival strategy but as she removes the costume, piece by piece, she becomes irrevocably committed to the fulfilment of her desire. Each film works in distinctive ways but these shared preoccupations, of landscape and of masquerade, return time and again, creating specific narrative inflections and underlining both of the central characters' conflicts and struggles.

High Tide

High Tide was made in Australia in 1987 with the assistance of the Australian Film Commission. It brought Gillian Armstrong and actress Judy Davis (who plays Lilli) together again, eight years after the success of *My Brilliant Career*. There was a strong female presence in the production team, which included Sandra Levy as producer and Laura Jones as scriptwriter, as well as Annette Patterson and Julie Forster, as production co-ordinator and production manager respectively. The narrative centres on a mother's accidental reunion with her daughter whom she had abandoned as an infant following her partner's death. As Armstrong explains, the film was originally scripted for a male lead:

> Lilli was originally to have been a man who came back to find his daughter, Ally. We raised the money on that script, and a couple of months before we started shooting, when I'd just started casting, I had the feeling something was wrong. I thought, I'm sick to death of seeing alienated selfish modern men, how about we do it as a woman? I thought too, it would add a lot more to the story because there'd been a number of films, like *Paris, Texas* and *Paper Moon*, in which a man had been touched by a small child: I thought that making the central character the mother would make it tougher. Society doesn't condone a woman who's behaved in that way, who's abandoned her baby.[2]

In the event, Davis played the part superbly, with a keen, ironic sensibility, and won an AFI award for the role.

Performance

The opening sequence of the film establishes performance as a key theme; the shiny, shimmering background to the film's titles turns out to be a stage backdrop, as the camera pans rapidly, coming to rest on a modern, wanna-be Elvis and his three chorus girls, who burst into song to delighted screams from the audience. Lilli is a part of this roadshow but is unable to take it seriously and mocks Lester (Frankie J. Holden), her employer, mercilessly. Performance comes easily to her but does not satisfy or involve her: 'That's where you and I fall apart, isn't it?' accuses Lester. 'Cos what I think's essential, you think is boring.'

Talent quests, roadshows and strip-tease performances feature frequently in the narrative. The first time we meet Bet (played by Jan Adele) who is Ally's grandmother (Ally is played by Claudia Karvan) and has looked after her since Lilli left, she is in her caravan, making-up in the mirror, getting ready to sing that evening. Bet enters fully into the spirit of the show, her obvious enjoyment of performance contrasting clearly with Lilli's sardonic detachment. Bet's flirtation with cowboy Joe (Bob Purtell) is similarly light-hearted; when Col (her local lover, played by John Clayton) exacts revenge by ramming Joe's truck the following morning, she tells Joe cheerfully to send her the bill if he thinks it wasn't worth it.

The local roadhouse provides the venue for the stage shows and it is here that Ally, who has accompanied her grandmother, first catches sight of Lilli. Both Lilli and Ally are bored by their surroundings; Ally puts her head round the partition and watches Lilli, her face reflected in the textured glass. Later, she sees her mother in the café and, still unaware of the relationship, she smiles at her through a glass screen. Lilli now knows who Ally is and has been warned off by Bet; she snubs the youngster.

Curiosity leads Lilli to watch her daughter intently, and she crouches down in the shower block to peer under the door as Ally shaves her legs. Shortly afterwards, she watches her daughter's hands and face through the caravan window as Ally works on her surfboard. Repeatedly, Ally and Lilli see and watch each other through screens and windows; when Ally has finally learned the truth, and Lilli has provided some painfully honest answers, the child's tearful face is shown pressed against the inside of the car window. In this film, the glass, the partitions, the stage curtains, the windows and screen doors act as emotional filters; at key moments of both recognition and non-recognition, they help to distance the characters from each other and from the audience. Both Bet and Lilli have lied, Bet to Ally in claiming that her mother was dead and Lilli in changing her name and denying her attachment. The concealment and the denial that are part of their lives are signalled by these reflecting and obscuring surfaces as well as by their theatrical costumes and roadshow trappings. Masquerade has become a way of life.

Marginal existences
The film is set in the southern coastal town of Eden, New South Wales, with its caravan park, fish factory and local tavern. Bet and Ally live in a caravan and do the local ice-cream run. Bet also works in the fish factory. People come and go from such places and have tenuous ties; those who stay are affected by the seasonal availability of work. 'This is our last run,' Ally tells the children who wait for ice-creams, but only for the winter.

Lilli is a drifter and her arrival in Eden is not planned. Neither can she tell Ally where she lives: 'God, that's a good question. Sydney, I think.' She is established as itinerant and without focus. 'I don't know which way you're going to jump next,' says Bet, 'and I don't think you do either.' Later, she confesses to Bet: 'I've always thought that I lived a kind of adventurous, brave kind of a life but I haven't really. I've been a coward.'

There are movements and transitions in Ally's life, too, that prepare the way for her decision to leave with her mother. Her friendships are straining and she is moving to adulthood, with Bet alternately seeking to release and restrain her. Ally's reconciliation with Lilli is effectively located and played out in the small town with its transient community and its coastal caravan park; it is a perfect location, at the edge of the land, full of shiny, wet surfaces, like the rocks on the shore which the camera skates across in the opening sequences of the film or like the sea itself. A rapidly panning or tracking camera which turns the image to a blur is used repeatedly as an integral part of the film's visual style and it underlines the sense of movement, displacement and change.

Significantly, the beach is the setting for Ally's first confrontation with Lilli, following the revelation that this woman is her mother. 'My mother's dead!' she shouts at Lilli, and then races away; the camera pulls back and she is a small figure, running into the distance, along a huge expanse of sand. Shortly afterwards, she and Lilli are in the parked car, overlooking the headland; Lilli makes an attempt to explain the past and then there is a long shot of the car perched high on the cliff, followed by a pan to waves crashing on to the shore; there is a figure lying on a surfboard and then the camera tilts back up to the clifftop. As mother and daughter reach an emotional impasse, the landscape contextualises their pain and struggle, creating distance and isolation and a sense of precariousness.

Lilli promises nothing. Ally leaves with her, calling to her friends as she goes, 'I'm going away with my mother!' Her surfboard is stowed in the car, an emblem of her commitment to her dead father, who was also a keen surfer. Ally's love of surfing will link her (like her mother) to the margins, to the ebb and flow of the tide.

No absolutes
High Tide has been described by Verina Glaessner as a film which refuses 'to go for full-blown melodrama'.[3] Brian McFarlane and Geoff Mayer argue that, like many Australian films, it sits between Hollywood melodrama and the European art-film: 'The desire for a certain level of moral ambiguity and loose narrative causality points towards the European art-film while the basic situations and overall dramatic context invite emotional expectations associated with melodrama.'[4]

The film refuses easy answers and questions of blame and responsibility are left open to the end. Lilli is a sympathetic and complex character; Bet is a stolid, loving and perceptive guardian. When the break comes, it is Ally who insists on returning to tell her grandmother, while Lilli waits in the car. Their parting is filmed inside the fish factory, in near black and white tones, with wet reflections everywhere. Bet knows she has lost. 'We're going and we'll come back,' says Ally, tearfully. As she leaves, the camera stays with Bet, standing beside a pile of fish crates, a lone, bulky figure, clad in a factory apron. There is a shot of Ally walking to the car, then a cut to the plastic strip curtain that hangs across the entrance of the factory, like a stage backdrop. The shiny curtain parts, and Bet's head and shoulders appear in the opening; then the camera pulls away rapidly and unevenly, into a long shot, and her figure diminishes. She is left, standing on the factory platform, receding quickly into the distance. The shot could be Ally's point of view, from the car, but there is no reverse shot of the girl to confirm this.

There is a further refusal to indulge the more sentimental spectator in the final moments of the film when Lilli has second thoughts. Having sent Ally into the restaurant ahead of her, she returns to the car and starts the engine. She looks towards Ally and the camera cuts to the child's small figure, once more filmed through a window. The viewer is left in suspense until the circling, hand-held camera approaches Ally from behind – and Lilli clasps her daughter. This

Ally (Claudia Karvan) and her nan (Jan Adele) in *High Tide*
Still courtesy of BFI STILLS, POSTERS AND DESIGNS

final hesitation and the mother's uncertainty set the film apart from its melodramatic ancestors; there is no emotional closure in this world and no confirmation of conventional values. The final, fast tracking shot of a shiny road with its vanishing white lines again emphasises movement and restlessness, and the vulnerability of the characters' lives.

The Piano

Of all the films discussed in this book, *The Piano* is certainly the best known. With its three Oscars and three British Academy Awards, it put Jane Campion in the top directors' league. The film won her the Palme d'Or at Cannes (the first time ever it had been won by a woman) and was widely acclaimed. Holly Hunter gave an award-winning performance as Ada, a Victorian Scotswoman whose father has arranged her marriage to Stewart (played by Sam Neill) and sent her to join him in New Zealand. Ada has a nine-year-old illegitimate daughter, Flora (Anna Paquin), who accompanies her.

Not all who saw the film liked it, however, and, perhaps more than most successful feature films, it seems to mean quite different things to different audiences. Detractors of the film have taken exception variously to Harvey Keitel's accent, to anomalies in the narrative and to the film's perceived 'pretentiousness'.[5] There has also been some disquiet among Maori about the way they are represented in the film.

Interestingly, and like *High Tide*, the film has links with the art-house tradition (with its Victorian costumes and sweeping landscapes) but it is also distinctively Australasian in its concerns. New Zealand and Australia have both claimed it as their own; development money came from Australia (the Australian Film Commission and the New South Wales Film and Television Office) and the production was funded by France. In the context of this book, the film is a good example of the cultural cross-fertilisation that occurs from one side of the Tasman to the other. Campion herself diplomatically describes it as an Australian production of a New Zealand story made with French finance.[6]

We noted earlier that Sybylla's story in *My Brilliant Career* owed a narrative debt to the Victorian novel *Jane Eyre*, and the Brontë sensibility has been mentioned, too, in connection with *The Piano*.[7] As a spirited and determined heroine who refuses to accept the conventional solution, Ada has by this time many predecessors in Australasian women's cinema.

The politics of voice
The first image of the film is of the light filtering through Ada's fingers; as she peeps through, we see what she sees, a fleshy pink curtain in front of the world. A childlike voice on the sound track explains, 'The voice you hear is not my speaking voice but my mind's voice. I have not spoken since I was six years old. No one knows why.' We are immediately inside Ada's world, seeing as she sees and listening to her mind. It is an enigmatic beginning to a powerful film which raises many questions about silence, language and oppression. Both in its cinematic form and in its thematic and narrative concerns, it explores modes of experience and expression which are beyond language itself.

Ada's silence is not imposed nor is it quite freely chosen; she is unconscious of its origins. Her father describes her silence as 'a dark talent' and Ada herself acknowledges that, in the end, silence affects everyone. She does not, she tells us, think of herself as silent because of her piano. She articulates her relationship to the world through her piano, as well as through her sign language, her daughter's voice, her notes and inscriptions, her mind's voice, with her own body, and through her silence. Her silence marks out a private space, puts a responsibility on others to 'listen' to her and ultimately to rethink their own relationships with the world. When Flora asks about her natural father, Ada says she 'could lay thoughts on his mind like a sheet'; they did not marry because, she says, he became frightened and stopped listening. Stewart is a frightened man, too, clumsy and authoritarian but also sympathetic and confused. Anxiously, he scans her face for the smallest signs of concession. Several times, he suggests they might start again but he is slow to learn. It is Baines (Harvey Keitel), the illiterate, who really listens and who learns about Ada through her music. When Stewart discovers Baines and Ada making love, he watches as if fascinated, first through a crack in the door and then from underneath the floorboards. His attempted rape of Ada and his inability to respond to her advances are further evidence of perversion and disturbance. Finally, he does hear what he imagines to be Ada's voice asking him to let her go, to let Baines try and save her; at last, and too late, having mutilated the body he could not own, he hears her and releases her: 'I want to wake up and find this was all a dream.'

In much feminist discourse, silence is equated with oppression or with absence. Exhortations to 'break the silence' (about rape, for example) or to retrieve and write 'herstory', as opposed to history, are founded on assumptions about the nature of silence as masking what could be present, as signalling an absence. In an interesting article about the film,[8] Valerie Hazel agrees that feminism generally regards silence as a negative condition and that it is rare to find an acknowledgement that silence may not be inevitably unhealthy and oppressive. In her reading of *The Piano*, however, she explores the notion of silence as an operation of power, as one mode of articulation and one form of attachment among others. Silence does not equal absence or passivity but it does not necessarily equal empowerment either and, if this is so, then neither does voice. The voice can no longer be thought of as giving automatic access to an identity, as a transparent link between the self and the world.

Masquerade
Just as silence is used strategically in the film, as one mode of articulation among others, so costume also becomes an operation of power. Initially, we are struck by the extreme inappropriateness of Ada's costume for her new surroundings. Hands reach up towards the camera as she and her daughter are lifted high and carried ashore from the canoe, through pounding surf. Beyond the beach, the mud is thick and grey; the long hooped skirts and petticoats, the dainty laced boots are hopelessly inadequate for this terrain. Ada and Flora repeatedly sink into the wet mud and dense, tangled vines pull at them from above. Shortly after their arrival, Ada is obliged to appear with Stewart in a wedding photograph; even though there will be no ceremony, there must be a photograph and Ada is dressed as a bride, to sit in torrential rain while the formality is completed. Once back indoors, drenched and angry, she rips off the bridal gown and storms from the room.

Costume is an encumbrance but it also affords some protection; Ada's and Flora's bonnets frame their pale, hostile faces in close-up against the grey skies, like emphatic circles. While they wait on the beach for Stewart to arrive, Ada's hooped crinoline petticoat forms a small enclosure, a tiny tent, which encircles them both. When Stewart later attempts to rape Ada, he pulls her down into the grey mud; he rips at her costume but the many layers afford her some protection as she tears at the branches and vines above her. Most significantly, in the bargain with Baines, Ada uses her costume to recover her beloved piano, one visit for every black key. Like a game of strip poker, each visit sees the removal of a new part of her costume, giving Baines access to a new part of her body – but also bringing Ada closer to her desire.

Mother (Holly Hunter) and daughter (Anna Paquin) in *The Piano*
Still courtesy of BFI STILLS, POSTERS AND DESIGNS

That costume is an operation of power is borne out, too, by the local Maori's adoption (and adaptation) of Victorian dress, Ada's shawl for instance, or the top hat. European costume connotes power; it is significant that it is Baines who rejects these fashions in favour of tattoos and a lifestyle which brings him closer to his Maori neighbours. It is also significant that Maori spectators of the shadow-play respond to the actors' costumes as 'real' and see beyond the fancy dress to the threat which the costume denies.

In Freudian terms, masquerade effectively conceals the castration threat posed by the woman; even little Flora's angel wings, which she wears again in the final movement of the film, long after the pantomime is over, may be read as an ironic denial of her power in the Oedipal-type struggle. It is Flora, after all, who delivers her mother's message of love, inscribed on a piano key, to Stewart and not to Baines as she had been instructed, with disastrous consequences. The use of dress and costume to conceal and to deny power is also reminiscent of *High Tide*, where, as we noted above, Lilli and Bet are both engaged in performance and masquerade, and both engaged, too, in forms of denial.

'How do they even know it's theirs?'
Issues of power and status are also explored in the film through its images of colonisation. Stewart, as Victorian patriarch and immigrant, embodies the imperial impulse; he is contemptuous of Maori custom and belief and tries to pay them for their work in buttons. When they refuse to sell their sacred land to him, he offers them guns. 'What do they want the land for?' he demands angrily. After all, he claims, they don't do anything with it, they don't cultivate it or burn it back. How do they even know it belongs to them?

Stewart's relationship to the land is in clear contrast to the local Maori way of life; for him, the land is simply a potential source of immediate profit and ripe for exploitation; it is an entitlement. He chops down trees and hacks his way through the vines and the mud, clearing the bush from the land, preparing for settlement.

His approach to Ada is similarly brutal and confused. Not understanding how much her piano means to her, he interprets her make-believe 'piano' (the keys of which she has carved on to the kitchen table) as a sign that she may be 'brain affected'; when he has seen his wife with Baines, his reaction is to tear her down too, to rape her and tame her, just like the land. David Eggleton remarks that in this film 'faces loom like landscapes';[9] neither Ada nor the land can expect to have self-sovereignty.

Stewart has a perverted and repressed sexuality (the Maori nickname for him is 'old dry balls') and there are clear associations made between his colonial and sexual identities. Baines, on the other hand, is relaxed in the natural environment, self-aware and sensitive by comparison. Though he, too, exploits Ada, and effectively colonises her body, he is not without tenderness; at night, in the half-light, alone and naked, he dusts the piano with his shirt and caresses it in her absence.

Baines shares his living space with the Maori, speaks their language and appreciates their traditions. He interprets what they say for Stewart, laughs with them at their jokes. Campion explores these aspects of colonisation too, of the contact between diverse cultures and of the effects of this contact. A group of Maori women sing a brief refrain from 'God Save the Queen'; others are puzzled by the pantomime; some of them don bits of the Victorian costume, a hat or a shawl.

In this film, we have images of colonisation which are sexual, political and ideological, worked through at several levels of the narrative. The struggles between those with power and those with less power, their negotiations and compromises, their strategies for survival and resistance, are explored in detail. In the context of displacement and isolation, these struggles become heightened and acute. When, in the early part of the film, Ada and Flora go back to the beach where the piano still stands, they temporarily escape both from Stewart and the hostile terrain; bathed in warm orange and yellow tones, that contrast markedly with the blue-greys of the bush and the mud further inland, Ada plays her piano and Flora dances in her petticoats on the beach. They are watched from a distance by a bemused Baines. As the light fades and the colours turn cooler, they return towards the cliff; the camera pulls back and, in a long aerial shot, we see their tracks on the sand and beside them a giant sea-horse made of shells; it is a memorable image, the sea-horse a symbol of creativity and female resourcefulness in a hostile world. Finally, it is Ada's will that saves her from drowning, that sees her comfortably installed with Baines in suburbia. But then her mind's voice returns to tell us that, at night, she still thinks of her piano in its silent, ocean grave; she thinks of herself 'floating above it', and we are left with a sense of her continued displacement; despite her new surroundings, she seems estranged now from life itself.

10

The Wave Rolls On

The 1990s have witnessed a new mood in Australasian women's film-making. It is a mood of confidence and strength and it stems from two roots: the feminist impulse of 1970s film-makers and the politics of identity in the 1980s, with its demand for a diversity of representations from the margins. This dual legacy is apparent in recent films, particularly in the films made by women of colour and lesbians, and it is to be celebrated, given the systematic exclusion or misrepresentation of black and homosexual characters from commercial cinema for most of the hundred years of its history.

The increase in the number of films coming from the experience of indigenous peoples in both Australia and New Zealand was discussed earlier, a development which throughout the 1980s saw women in the vanguard. In this chapter, we shall be looking at films in which issues of race and racism interface with issues of sex and sexuality as well as examining the impact of lesbian film-making around issues of 'otherness'. We shall also include discussion of some of the most recent films from both New Zealand and Australia which continue the tradition of the women's wave, by picking up its familiar key concerns of ethnicity, the family and the land.

The Background

Over the last two decades, debates around the question of gender, spearheaded internationally by gay politics, have been crucial in both academic and popular culture. Theorists, artists and the media have focused on sex and the taboos that surround it. The prevailing mood has been a fascination with sexual transgression and gender trespass which, while having a down-side (a reaction against both feminism and left-wing politics as 'politically correct'), has allowed for a more progressive challenge to be mounted against the structures that fix us in positions of oppression. Ways of perceiving social formations are changing and many contemporary films, especially those made by women, are reflecting this change. Australasian short films are exemplary in this respect.

Three Short Films

The confidence of Australasian women film-makers today that we have already referred to can be illustrated by three short films, made in the early 1990s, which link questions of race with the positioning of women in society. The twin issues of racism and sexism are represented in all three films in a fresh and original manner. Subjects which, twenty years ago, would have been approached with seriousness and caution are here handled playfully, even humorously. This new generation of film-makers is also much more inclined to foreground female pleasure and to focus on the role of memory, fantasy and desire in the struggle against oppression. The collective message of these three films is to stress the importance of imagination, as well as action, in the challenge to racism and sexism. Apart from the shared preoccupations of these films and the fact that each has a woman as the central character, whose ethnicity (to a greater or lesser extent) sets her apart from mainstream society, it is interesting to note that all three films have been in receipt of official funding.

Mokopuna (Wheta Fala, 1992, New Zealand, 6 mins) was funded by the Creative Film Fund of the (then) Queen Elizabeth II Arts Council of New Zealand, the New Zealand Film Commission and Television New Zealand. Its impact depends on its punchline, so to speak; namely that its central character, a Maori woman called Mere, turns out to be, in fact, the Prime Minister of New Zealand. The title, *mokopuna*, is the Maori word for grandchild or descendant and the film's main point of reference is the female Maori experience; Maori language is used in the film and, through Mere's eyes, a contrast is drawn between the past and the present, between the bush and the urban landscape of modern Wellington.

The film follows Mere on her journey to work. Shot in black and white, it plays on the central mystery that surrounds her, as she emerges from a palatial house from behind wrought-iron gates (bearing the word '*mokopuna*'), dressed in smart European clothes. As she begins to walk down the path, a car pulls up, driven by a young Maori woman wearing sunglasses and speaking into a mobile phone. Mere walks past the car and the driver starts to trail her. Making her way through the busy city streets, Mere gets flashbacks of the past, sequences of a barefooted pregnant woman struggling through the undergrowth and speaking in (untranslated) Maori, the sound of gun shots in the distance.

During Mere's journey, more memories come flooding back and the film cuts between the present and the past, making clear contrasts. At one point, Mere smudges lipstick on to her chin, as if she is reflecting on the traditional practice of 'moko' or tattooing, and she says, in English, 'Clay will not cling to iron.' Her memories of the hardships of early Maori life are memories of women and of the land. Her journey to work becomes a journey into her ancestral past; she is *mokopuna*, struggling to recall. There are shots of a Maori woman carrying shopping along a sunny suburban street; she is a mother admonishing a child, speaking directly to the camera, and to Mere, we assume. And as the adult Mere approaches her destination, she seems also to remember the identity of the pregnant woman in the bush: 'Mere was the one who saved our line and I'm her namesake.' A shot of a land rights demonstration by Maori activists and, on the sound track, a voice urgently calling 'Mum!', underline the need for her not to forget her past or her culture. The importance of her personal identity, of the generations of Maori women who are her ancestors, and her people's history is then acknowledged by Mere: 'I won't forget.' As she arrives at the office, the female chauffeur is waiting and a Pakeha doorman greets her in Maori, addressing her as 'Prime Minister'; the camera pulls back and tilts up to the beehive dome of the central government building.

The links made in *Mokopuna* between the individual and her culture also resonate in an Australian short called *Yeah, Mostafa!* (Ali Higson, 1993, 11 mins). Funded by the Australian Film Commission, it revolves round the character of Annette who, like Mere, is a middle-aged woman caught between two cultures, in this case the Arabic and the Australian. She experiences marginalisation from both sides. Her upbringing and her marriage have completely westernised her; she is cut off from her (supposed) Lebanese roots. Whether Annette is Lebanese or simply 'feels' Lebanese is unclear in the film, but she is experiencing an identity crisis, perhaps a mid-life crisis, too. At home, her life is empty and joyless. She is dominated by a slobbish husband and an equally slobbish brother who (in the film) represent mainstream

Australian culture. By contrast, the Arabic men who work in the night-club which represents Annette's escape route (she is a belly dancer there) are represented as being in tune with life and its rhythms. The club, an exciting and exotic place, full of colour, dance and throbbing Middle Eastern music, is set in opposition to Annette's home, where the men get drunk and watch pornographic videos.

Filmed in wonderfully vibrant colours, the film's use of interiors (compared with the exteriors used in *Mokopuna*) and mysterious decor (curtains, veils and smoke, as well as objets d'art, finger cymbals and pearl necklaces) constructs a site of fantasy and eroticism.

The central discourse is female. A group of women, Annette's Lebanese 'sisters', discuss culture, men and marriage on the sound track, over images of a magical world, deserted beaches, grottos, and orange flame fires. The Arabic music constructs a sense of the dreamlike, the beat being almost subliminal in its effects. While cultural difference is celebrated in the film, Annette, who aspires to free herself from her particular form of captivity, makes it clear that she understands women of all cultures are kept in subservience, that she feels for (and at one with) the women behind the veil.

Representing 'difference' as marginal and colourful is also a feature of writer/director Monica Pellizzari's film *Just Desserts* (1993, Australia, 12 mins). Like *Yeah, Mostafa!* this film contrasts a vibrant culture, this time Mediterranean, with the dominant, white Australian culture but it uses food as a motif for representing difference where *Yeah, Mostafa!* uses mise-en-scène and music. Pellizzari's preoccupation with her Italian origins is also explored in an earlier film, *Rabbit on the Moon*, which visualises the world from a child's point of view, and again in a later film (her first feature) called *Fistful of Flies* (1996). *Just Desserts* is a rites-of-passage film, looking at the development from childhood to adolescence of Maria Stroppi, its central character.

The film is structured in a series of episodes, titled after the Italian culinary concoctions that we see Maria's mother preparing throughout the film. Each dish (and episode) corresponds to a crucial moment in Maria's sexual development. The episodes are divided between the black and white footage that represents Australian reality, shot with dialogue in semi-social-realist mode, and colour footage to construct the Mediterranean magical realism. The sound track for these latter sequences uses Italian music, both operatic and religious. The implicit value judgement between these contrasting worlds is further emphasised by the use of cross-cutting, split screen and even multiple images within the frame.

The contrasting images are used to ironic and very funny effect. One notable example is the 'Gnocchi' episode where we see Maria's mother cutting up dumplings from a tubular roll of pastry, intercut with Maria losing her virginity to her boyfriend on the beach, not a very pleasurable or memorable experience for Maria; the dumplings are far more successful!

The mother's cooking, a crucial activity in Italian family life, becomes the link and symbol of the female cultural tradition. The food takes on a life of its own, particularly in the final episode called 'The Pizzas are Sleeping' where Maria's mother places her pizzas on Maria's bed waiting for them to rise, while Maria lies anxiously, waiting for her period to come. Other memorable moments include Maria and her friend Mona discovering masturbation, while mother cooks Friole Veneti or Venetian fritters that are shaped like little vaginas. Female sexuality is further explored by the two friends in the episode 'Polenta' where Maria and Mona 'get married' and are enjoying a conjugal kiss until Mona's mother drags her daughter home, blaming Maria for her bad influence and making racist innuendos. Meanwhile, Maria remembers her auntie in Italy who was a lesbian and never got married.

The opposition Maria experiences from mainstream society both to her culture and her fledgling sexuality are clearly connected in this film and while its mood is predominantly comic, like the other two films discussed here, it packs a strong political punch. All three films link a concern with race or ethnicity to that of gender roles, dealing with the position of women within the state, the culture and the family. With the growth of film-making by women from (in the Australian context) Southern Europe and (in the New Zealand context) from Western Samoa and the Pacific Islands, such strong female representations are continuing the tradition begun in the 1980s with films such as *Serious Undertakings* and *Shadow Panic*. As we have suggested, the difference between women's films then and now lies in the approach to the subject, which in turn is influenced by the fact that many contemporary women film-makers come from the margins rather than the mainstream, and from particular subject positions.

National Differences

Despite the commonality and the shared preoccupations, such as the concern to link race or ethnicity to gender, there continue to be interesting differences between films coming out of Australia and New Zealand. The cinematic traditions of the respective women's waves can be described (at the risk of generalising) as, for Australia, a darkly ironic interest in family dysfunctionality within the suburban context and, for New Zealand, the feminist reworking of psychodrama. Though the interchange of ideas and talent between the two countries means that strict definitions and distinctions may not always be appropriate, feature films that may be cited to illustrate the point are, for Australia, *Celia* and *The Last Days of Chez Nous*, and for New Zealand, *Trial Run* and *Crush*.

It is worth briefly focusing on the developments in women's filmmaking along these lines. We turn first to psychodrama as a thread that runs through New Zealand women's film-making and look at how contemporary film-makers are continuing to use this genre to explore issues of sexuality.

NZ feminist psychodrama
The psychodrama's continuing popularity among New Zealand's women film-makers may well be due to the ambiguous representation of female friendships which is a feature of the genre and which gives young lesbian film-makers some reference points for their work. For example, the hints of a polymorphous perversity between Rosemary and Frances in *Trial Run* and the suggested lesbianism between Christina and Lane in the opening narrative sequence of *Crush*, followed by Lane's blatant bisexuality and play with gender roles throughout the film are signposts to the development of much more overt lesbian representations in later films.

We noted that the fascination with sexual taboos is a contemporary trend; it has always been a feature of psychodrama and, to a lesser extent, its more mainstream Hollywood cousin, the psychological thriller. As noted previously, the feminist reworking of the psychodrama has taken a number of forms, for example from a kind of role reversal in *Trial Run* where Rosemary moves from female in distress to investigative hero, to phallic female in *Crush* where Lane moves from female friend to femme fatale. In both films, the female characters function to blur the categories of the mainstream genre, while still remaining at some level trapped in their original roles.

The potential of psychodrama for exploring sexualised female friendships has been exploited in a number of New Zealand films and defined as the central enigma in a number of narratives. Sally Smith's

Time Trap (1991, New Zealand, 17 mins) is a case in point. In this film, the classic woman in distress is also the final champion. She is one half of a lesbian couple who are simultaneously going through personal crises. It is interesting to note that Melanie Read, the director of *Trial Run*, had a big input into the film. Credited as editor, sound editor and production adviser, she was also instrumental in getting the film completed after Sally Smith's untimely death, five months after the filming.

Sally Smith's brief film-making career provides a crucial link between the feminist concerns of the 1970s and the more overt lesbian representations of the late 1980s and early 1990s. In her work, the politics of the women's movement combine with the more erotic preoccupations of contemporary women's films. Her earlier short film, *Life in the Kitchen* (1988, 7 mins) shows a woman escaping the drudgery of her traditional role by fantasising. The film is described as follows: 'A woman alone in her kitchen surrounded by dirty dishes and overflowing ashtrays, fantasises about a sensual lesbian encounter where naked women roll in paint, play with fruit and intertwine with one another.'[1] *Time Trap* continues the contemporary trend towards the exploration of the power of the female imagination, but it also touches upon concerns that are part of the legacy of feminism. For example, Sally Smith was interested in the notion of 'herstory' and her narrative links the concerns of women in the present with those from the past. Moreover, the film is also an attempt to construct a strong image of solidarity among women (at least at the end of the film), women who would otherwise be divided because of differences in age and class.

Time Trap is shot in black and white and tells the story of a female couple, Sheryl and Lynn, signalled to some extent as 'butch' and 'femme', who move into a rambling, derelict house together. Lynn, in a sense, becomes the woman in distress because she experiences a number of weird episodes and is haunted by strange scenes when she is alone in the house. Atmospherically, the film contains all the elements of a gothic horror; iconographically, there is moonlight, thunderstorms, dream imagery and things that go bump in the night. This is underlined by the effects and the cinematography (strange angles, low-key lighting, steadicam tracks and so on). The sound track is ghostly and there is very little dialogue.

On their arrival, the women encounter a strange, old woman who shambles about with a gun and a sack on her back, catching rats. As they enter the house, Lynn's pet cat does a runner. While Lynn is being spooked, Sheryl is being sensible and their relationship becomes increasingly strained. Gradually, they get to know the old bag lady, Mavis, and the central mystery of the place begins to unfold. Lynn gets inadvertently caught up in the old woman's strong memories and, at certain moments, becomes literally trapped in the old woman's past, the 'time trap' of the title. The replaying of Mavis's trauma, a violent incident involving a man attacking her with a poker which is reminiscent of a 'below-stairs' Victorian melodrama, is finally resolved when Lynn saves her by grabbing the poker and beating the man.

The second crucial 'haunting' of the film is the old woman's memory of a cherished moment with her dead daughter whom, in her mind, she identifies as Lynn. These are uncanny moments and resolution is finally achieved when the three women communicate with one another over tea and cake. At this point, the couple, Lynn and Sheryl, are reunited, Mavis becomes a friend and the cat returns. The film is an impressive and strangely beautiful reworking of the 'woman as victim' theme. Its mood of threat and menace is constructed out of what can be imagined and what is remembered. Lynn, although threatened, becomes the agent for the laying of the sexually violent ghost and, through her resemblance to the old woman's daughter and her unconscious desire to connect with her love, she becomes the beacon of hope for all of them. Made with money from the Arts Council of New Zealand, the film carries the following dedication: 'Sally Smith, maker of *Time Trap*, died of cancer five months after the filming. She will be missed as a woman film maker, a woman photographer, a friend, a lover.'

Another very intense New Zealand short film which uses psychodrama and is visually expressive, with sound effects but no dialogue, is Christine Jeff's *Stroke* (1993, 8 mins), a film which she both wrote and directed and which was selected for both Cannes and the Sundance festivals. Like *Crush*, its title is ambiguous and conflict is again a strong feature of the film. Like *Time Trap*, its horror is based on suspense and the anxiety and fear experienced by the central and, in this case, lone female. The threat in this film has been pared down to an almost symbolic set of oppositions. Its power is constructed through its strong visualisation, its pace, colour and sound. The opening sequence of the film involves a woman alone in a swimming pool. Bathed in blue light and clad in a flowery swimsuit and bathing cap, she is shown floating tranquilly in the water. Suddenly out of the blue (literally), the film cuts to a team of male swimmers, dressed identically in purposeful striped trunks, tight caps and goggles. They appear as an alien, almost robotic presence as they dive in formation into the pool.

At this point, the pace quickens and we cut from the startled woman to the pack of men who pump and thrust their way through the water making directly for her. The lighting changes from blue to red and the horror scenario begins to unfold. The camera has lingered on the men's genital areas as they prepare to dive into the pool and the sexual threat is clearly established as they plough towards the woman. The visualisation of the swimming team as terminators, mindless and destructive, is enhanced by optically reprinted images, an abrupt change of pace and by jangling music and heavy breathing. The woman turns and begins to swim towards them, as though to cut them off, a lone female with feminine attributes of grace, self-sufficiency and intuition pitted against a team of men with masculine attributes of power, competitiveness and blind instinct. The film cross-cuts between them and the suspense builds as they move towards collision. Then, at the final moment, the woman launches herself over them and swims to safety. Like the final girl in a slasher movie,[2] she has allayed the threat by outwitting the mindless posse. The final sequence of the film has the woman alone once more, floating tranquilly in the blue water.

Australian tendencies
If the psychodrama emerges as the dominant genre for New Zealand women film-makers, then it is the representation of suburban family dysfunctionality that seems to be the preoccupation of their Australian sisters. In this respect, Ana Kokkinos's *Only the Brave* (1994) provides a powerful illustration, concerned as it is with a number of familiar issues including the experience of young girls growing up in damaging families, ethnic difference and female sexuality.

Only the Brave is a feature-length film made with the support of the Women's Programme of the Australian Film Commission, telling the story of Alex (Elena Mandalis), a Greek-Australian teenager, who has a close friendship with schoolmate Vicki (Dora Kaskanis), also of Greek origin. Both girls are deeply troubled. Alex is obsessed by the memory of her mother who has left the family home and Vicki, who lives in a 'normal' nuclear family, is being abused by her father. Their resulting alienation manifests itself in Alex in a retreat into dreams and fantasy and in Vicki, the more deeply damaged of the two, in violent and self-destructive behaviour. With two other girls from school, they form a gang and generally break the rules by smoking, drinking, messing around with boys and, more seriously, by starting fires on the outskirts of the town.

The film is shot in muted colours. Many of the sequences are filmed at night against an industrial landscape of high-rise buildings, factory chimneys, belching smoke and run-down warehouses. The locations are stark and the mood of the film is dark and hard-edged. The only visual relief to the night-time blue is provided by the strong red and orange of the flames from the fires started by the girls. The opening sequence sets the tone. A desolate area on the fringes of suburbia provides the site for the arsonist activity: run-down, graffiti-sprayed sheds, the lights of the town, the roar of traffic passing overhead on concrete highways, the sound of the trains on the railway passing in the distance. This is an urban wasteland and the girls are lost, stranded souls.

In a derelict railway siding, Alex and Vicki meet and endlessly discuss running away. Alex wants to go to Sydney to search for her missing mother, whom she constantly sees in daydreams, shown as flashbacks. The strong visions are always of a beautiful woman wearing a red dress, often drunk, to whom the child, Alex, runs. These moments of memory, fantasy and desire strongly recall the images in the short film *Swimming*, also about a missing mother. Vicki, on the other hand, simply wants to escape. Their friendship and their shared intensity is always on the edge of a physical relationship. But they, like all the characters in the film, are in deep denial about their feelings, and Vicky, whose persona is highly sexualised, encourages Alex to have sex with her boyfriend. Since her tentative advances are rejected by Vicki, Alex is drawn to her English teacher, a woman who seems uncertain herself about her sexuality. Recognising Alex's passion for writing, she takes her to a poetry reading at a bar in the town. But in *Only the Brave*, no adult is reliable; having touched Alex's desire, the teacher later rebuffs her, after bringing her home to her flat. She puts Alex up in the spare room for the night.

Alex's relationship with her father is similarly volatile. He attempts a closeness and is seemingly benign, a relaxed middle-aged Australian biker. But he deceives Alex about the situation with her mother and tries to conceal the information he has about her. Alex's desire for intimacy and for love are grasped only in fleeting moments with Vicki. Together, they share a fantasy; as Alex verbalises a scene in which Vicki is constructed as a beautiful and adored singing star, Vicki

Alex (Elena Mandalis) in fighting form in *Only the Brave*
Still courtesy of BFI STILLS, POSTERS AND DESIGNS

makes her entrance, wearing Alex's mother's red dress. They act out this euphoric moment in the bedroom until Alex's father interrupts them. He is confused. He has no idea what his daughter thinks and feels and there is an enormous gulf between them.

Tortured by her memories and confused by her sexuality, things begin to reach a climax when Alex is beaten up in the school toilets by a rival gang leader who accuses her of being a lesbian. In this incident, Alex's gang members, including Vicki, betray her. Later that night, Alex catches sight of Vicki through her window. She is being raped by her father. Alex tries to get help from the English teacher but to no avail. Vicki sets fire to the school library and then to herself. Alex tries to save her and ends up in hospital with burns.

In the hospital bed, Alex is withdrawn and refuses to acknowledge the presence of either her father or her teacher. Finally, her mother is there in the room, a long take of the woman Alex has longed for. She holds the gaze but cannot make any contact. She does not speak to her or even touch her. There is an abrupt cut.

In the final sequence, we see Alex hang her mother's red dress up on a wire fence. It is her last gesture before leaving. The last image of the film shows her in long shot, a tiny figure walking an endless road.

The power of this film lies in its superb visualisation of anger and pain, desire and passion, in its convincing performances from a cast of non-professional actors (whom the director rehearsed for five months before filming) and, finally, in its central portrayal of Alex, whose resilience against the odds places her in the category of 'the brave'. The film's message is an unremitting indictment of adults, of families, of teachers and of society as a whole.

Afterword

In conclusion, we want to refer to a crop of recent Australasian films, some features and some short dramas, which continue the tradition of the women's wave. This wave, as we have identified it, is characterised by those films made by women about women that are crucially preoccupied with one or more of the following issues: the land, the family and racial difference.

Margot Nash's debut feature *Vacant Possession* (1995) is exemplary in all the defining aspects. It was directed and scripted by Nash and made with the assistance of the Women's Programme of the Australian Film Commission. Margot Nash's film-making career, like her film, is in many ways typical. Like many of the women film-makers we have discussed, Nash moved into the field from other artistic media; in her case, she had had experience in both acting and still photography. Her earlier films include both documentaries and short experimental dramas.[3] In so spectacularly exemplifying the Australasian women's wave, her film *Vacant Possession* provides a fitting epilogue for this book and, as such, it will be discussed in some detail. To date, it is still awaiting British distribution.

The film deals with land issues both in terms of rights (Aboriginal ancestral rights) and in terms of ecology (treating the land with respect, not poisoning or plundering it, for instance). Again, like many of the other films we have discussed, the narrative is woven around the drama of a family which is almost classically dysfunctional: a deranged and violent father, ineffectual and adoring mother, sisters who are rivals. Through the protagonist Tessa (Pamela Rabe), the film constructs a number of female points of view, from young girl to adolescent to adult. Tessa's white nuclear family, ruled by the father, is contrasted unfavourably with the Aboriginal extended family headed by Auntie Beryl (a supportive and expansive matriarch).

The film opens with a dream. In a night-time shot, we glide through a blue-lit mangrove swamp. The mood is primeval and timeless and it is a moment we return to throughout the film. There is a cut to a day-time shot of the sea. A small boat is sailing across Botany Bay. Tessa (in the present), a woman in her thirties, is sitting at the prow trailing her hand in the water. Her voice-over provides the narrative opening. She is returning home after the death of her mother to claim her inheritance – the small wooden house named 'Irene', where she grew up. During the last lap of her journey home, Tessa is sitting in her sister Kate's car, being driven along the bay. There is a palpable tension between them. Tessa notices an unpleasant smell. The bay is being dredged and poisonous mercury deposits are being unearthed. The brief almost inconsequential dialogue will counterpoint Tessa's personal drama. The unfolding evidence that all is not well with the land begins to be linked to a legacy of colonial development. The white settlers have upset the balance between the land and the (indigenous) people. Millie (Auntie Beryl's granddaughter) has a white cat with no ears. He lost his ears because of cancer; the land and the creatures on it are ailing. The cat's name is 'Captain Cook'; Millie explains that, like his namesake, he arrived uninvited.

The film's narrative works like a jigsaw puzzle. The whole picture is constructed from a patchwork of diverse elements. Tessa, once she has moved back to 'Irene', begins to find the missing pieces of her life which will help her to understand the person she is. She ran away when she was 16 and, on her return, the past comes flooding back both to haunt and enlighten her in the form of dreams, reveries, half-buried memories and the reappearance of people she once knew. In a sense, Millie provides the link and stimulates the remembering: the warm musical mother; the manic, tortured father, a high-ranking scientist, crying over photos of his dead RAF comrades, still haunted by wartime trauma; Tessa herself, a sickly child, being comforted by her mother, comforting her father.

Margot Nash's prolific use of flashback is both a playing with time and a link with memory, in its therapeutic role. Tessa not only recalls her past but is physically positioned within it both as adult and child. She is thus able to address and comfort the child that is her, as for example when we see the girl Tessa weeping on the bed and the adult Tessa cradling her in her arms. Nash's film shows that as with political history, so with personal history; the past is always a part of our present and only through the past can we make sense of the present. Through flashbacks (Tessa's memories), the film reconstructs Tessa's teenage years, her youthful affair with Auntie Beryl's son Mitch, the violent reaction of her father when he learns she is pregnant, the resulting damage, Tessa's flight, Mitch's premature death.

The film's emotional climax is played out in the cellar between Tessa and her father, with an injured Millie lying in the candle-light, while a storm rages above them. A tentative truce is reached between Tessa and her father and a link is made between him and Millie when he promises to help the girl with her school project on the mangrove swamp, since his work as a government scientist has given him privileged information about the land. Most importantly of all, the problem of 'Irene' and Tessa's right to inherit it is unexpectedly resolved. Learning from her father that the land on which the house is built was Crown lottery land, effectively stolen from the Aboriginals, Tessa vows to give 'Irene' to Auntie Beryl and her family. She is rebuked by Millie: 'We don't want your house. Why do you white people think you always know what we want?'

In the end, Tessa gives up her claim to the house and, almost magically, receives her rightful inheritance, namely her mother's wedding ring. In a sleight of hand, she makes the ring disappear; it is an optical illusion, the same visual trick which, as Nash subtly suggests, is the very essence of cinema itself.

Two other Australian feature films, both made in 1996, are also worth a mention here, as further confirmation that the women's wave continues. Shirley Barrett's first feature film, *Love Serenade*, focuses on the relationship between two sisters. The film was produced by Jan Chapman (who was responsible for *The Last Days of Chez Nous* and *The Piano*) and was made with assistance from the Australian Film Finance Corporation. It won the Camera d'Or at Cannes in 1996.

The sisters, one of whom works in a Chinese restaurant and the other in the local hairdressing salon, live in a suburb that is characteristically surreal, and this small outback town, ironically called Sunray, provides the backdrop for the drama between them. Into town and into their lives comes Ken Sherry, a sleazy DJ from Melbourne whose arrival galvanises the latent rivalry between the sisters. Critically compared to *Sweetie* in its readiness to find something sinister in the mundane and the ordinary, *Love Serenade* is a funny, sad, warm and bizarre film. Memorable for its strange and audacious imagery (for instance, its use of fish as a visual motif) and for its absurdist ending, it sits comfortably in the dark Australian suburban drama that we have identified as a recurrent feature of recent Australian women's work. Shirley Barrett's screenplay wins the approval of film reviewer Sandra Hall: 'Scripts which break the rules of conventional narrative are almost a defining element of Australian cinema.'[4]

Another impressive feature dealing with sisters, family and the land (in terms of place) is Clara Law's *Floating Life* (1996). Set in the 1950s, the film deals with the experience of displacement, this time that of a Chinese family. When ageing parents from Hong Kong join their younger daughter, Bing, who resides in an Australian suburb, a comic nightmare which is both complex and moving begins to unfold. The emotional trauma that both parents and siblings undergo (the elder daughter lives in Munich and the brother still resides in Hong Kong) is based in the director's own experience. Born in Macau, brought up in Hong Kong, at film school in England and now resident in Australia, Clara Law is no stranger to the suffering of immigrants. She has described the film as providing a 'panorama of post-colonial identity'[5] and this is no empty boast. Shot across three continents, in Australia, Hong Kong and Germany, it is the first Australian film to deal with the Chinese diaspora and indeed, the first to use English subtitles. The film is an impressive achievement. Clara Law has a wealth of directorial experience, having directed four films in Hong Kong. She co-scripted *Floating Life* with her husband and collaborator Eddie

Fong, himself an experienced film editor. It is produced by Brigit Iken who was also responsible for *An Angel at My Table* and, in terms of distribution and exhibition, it extends the international market for Australian films, traditionally Europe and the USA, to Asia.

In spite of the vastness of its canvas, the film is very finely observed. Apart from the powerful representations of family relationships and ties, the particularities of the Australian suburban landscape are extraordinarily rendered, the bleached pastels of the afternoon light appearing positively surreal. About filming in Australia, Law remarks: 'The landscape is so very primeval here. Not unlike China in its ancient feel. But the air is so crisp, so fresh, that colours seem more pure.'[6]

Another excellent example of the way immigration is enriching and expanding the national cinema is provided by the Western Samoan film-maker, Sima Urale. Her recent short film *O Tamaiti* (*The Children*, 15 mins) was made in New Zealand with financial help from the Short Film Fund of the NZFC and it won awards as the best short film at both the Asia Pacific and the Venice International film festivals in 1996. Urale, whose parents emigrated to New Zealand when she was six, came to film-making (like Margot Nash) from a career in acting. As with many of the film-makers mentioned in this book, she gained her film training in Australia, at the Victorian College of the Arts in Melbourne. Like Clara Law, her personal experience of displacement and hardship as a member of a marginalised settler group within the mainstream culture has influenced her work. Of *O Tamaiti*, Sima Urale says: 'It is about the unconditional bond among children in Pacific Island families.'[7]

In fact, the film is shot almost completely from the children's points of view, with the camera placed at child's eye-level. The tragic drama revolves round a young boy, Tino, who is in charge of his four younger siblings. When another child is born, his burden becomes almost unbearable; then the baby dies of cot death. The parents are hardly seen but are heard giving instructions, arguing, making love. The absence of adults, and of white people, gives this film a unique quality. Urale chose to film in black and white in order 'to shed the stereotypical images of Pacific Islanders as a kitsch culture with colourful paraphernalia'.[8] The pathos of the film is poignantly depicted when finally Tino has to lead his small brothers and sisters out of the church because they are 'too noisy' for the baby's funeral. This tragic image of alienated and dejected children expresses the solidarity and the suffering that many immigrants experience.

Another New Zealand short film, *The Beach* (1996, 8 mins), which was made by Danish-born Dorthe Scheffmann with a grant from the Creative Film and Video Fund of New Zealand, provides a further fine example of the ways in which cultural diversity can enrich a national cinema. Filmed by Scheffmann's partner, cinematographer Stuart Dryburgh (who was an Oscar nominee for his work on *The Piano*), *The Beach* is visually stunning and has considerable narrative power.

The film opens with an atmospheric, long, slow track along a beach, the colour bleached out to a hot, hazy white, the frame almost emptied of objects, except for a few small knots of people dwarfed by the huge seascape. The visual quality is painterly, like an early impressionist canvas, and the mood is one of drowsy indolence. We see a young boy playing beach cricket with an adult (his father) and the camera comes to rest on two women, sunbathing on beach towels. They are obviously friends, perhaps even more than friends since there is an erotic tension between them that gives their relationship an ambiguous quality, reminiscent of Christina and Lane in *Crush*. As one of the women languidly and sensually rubs the other's shoulders with oil, she discovers a large bruise on her friend's side. It emerges that this woman (she is the mother of the boy playing cricket) is being battered by her husband. The friend calls the husband over and in the exchange that follows, he swears at her abusively. Quick as a flash and in a gesture that completely disrupts the film's languid pace, she leaps up and kicks him in the balls. The little boy watches it all and in the last moments of the film, we see him and his mother's friend splashing playfully in the sea; his final bemused expression, however, recalls Awatea, the watchful young girl in *Mauri*, another silent child observing an adult drama and learning.

It is clear from these most recent films that a significant number of women film-makers in both countries continue to share the preoccupations we have identified in earlier work by Australasian women, notwithstanding some national tendencies and some varying nuances and emphases. All the films discussed in this chapter and throughout the book share an interest in the female subject, as child, mother, grandmother, sister, wife, friend, worker, activist and lover. As a body of work, the combined representations of women from these Australian and New Zealand film-makers over the last two decades is arguably the most substantial contribution to women's cinema anywhere in the world.

The films we have discussed bear witness to a rich and varied input from a number of sources. Supported by a range of funding mechanisms, drawing on a legacy of a variety of filmic traditions and representing the influences of many different cultures, the Australasian women's wave is impressive and inspiring. We have enjoyed the films discussed in this book (and many others we have not had the scope to include). We have lived with them, learnt from them, laughed and cried with them and we wrote this book to pay tribute to them. Long may the wave roll!

Notes

1. The Back Drop (pp. 1–8)
1. 'Reflecting Reality: Gaylene Preston, An Interview', in J. Dennis and J. Bieringa (eds), *Film in Aotearoa New Zealand*, Wellington, Victoria University Press, 1992, p. 171.
2. A. Blonski, B. Creed and F. Freiberg (eds), *Don't Shoot Darling! Women's Independent Film-making in Australia*, Richmond Victoria, Greenhouse, 1987, p. 64.
3. A. Kuhn (ed.), *Women's Companion to International Film*, London, Virago, 1990, p. 63.
4. Ibid., p. 204.
5. Ibid., p. 63.
6. N. Rattigan, *Images of Australia: 100 Films of the New Australian Cinema*, Dallas, Southern Methodist University Press, 1991, p. 12.
7. J. Batten, 'Art and Identity', in D. Novitz and B. Willmott (eds), *Culture and Identity in New Zealand*, Wellington, GP Books, 1989, p. 219. (Note: a marae is a Maori meeting place, the centre of a Maori community.)
8. J. Jupp, 'Identity', in R. Nile (ed.), *Australian Civilisation*, Melbourne, Oxford University Press, 1994, p. 76.

2. Brilliant Beginnings (pp. 9–18)
1. The McDonagh sisters (Paulette, Isobel and Phyllis) directed a silent film called *The Cheaters* in 1926 (with a sound version in 1930). In all, they made four feature films, with a talkie called *Two Minutes Silence* appearing in 1934.
2. Notable titles include *Walkabout* (Nicolas Roeg, 1971), *The Cars That Ate Paris* (Peter Weir, 1974), *Storm Boy* (Henri Safran, 1977) and *The Chant of Jimmie Blacksmith* (Fred Schepisi, 1978).
3. N. Rattigan, *Images of Australia: 100 Films of the New Australian Cinema*, Dallas, Southern Methodist University Press, 1991, p. 17.
4. See, for example, *Jezebel* (William Wyler, 1938), *All This and Heaven Too* (Anatole Litvak, 1940), *Wuthering Heights* (William Wyler, 1940) and *Letter from an Unknown Woman* (Max Ophuls, 1948).
5. See Rattigan, *Images of Australia*, Introduction.

3. A New Zealand Landmark (pp. 19–29)
1. 'Melanie Read: De-victimising Women', interview by Tony Mitchell, *Filmviews*, vol. 31, no. 127, Autumn 1986, p. 127.
2. P. Cook (ed.), *The Cinema Book*, London, BFI, 1985, p. 105.
3. Ibid., p. 128.
4. L. Mulvey, 'Visual Pleasure and Narrative Cinema', *Screen*, vol. 16, no. 3, Autumn 1975.
5. R. Horrocks, 'Alternatives: Experimental Film Making in New Zealand', in J. Dennis and J. Bieringa (eds), *Film in Aotearoa New Zealand*, Wellington, Victoria University Press, 1992, pp. 68–75.

4. Short Circuits (pp. 30–45)
1. Gillian Armstrong's documentaries include, for example, *Not Just a Pretty Face* (Australia, 1983); Merata Mita's documentary film *Patu!* (New Zealand, 1983) is discussed briefly in Chapter 5.
2. B. Alysen, 'Australian Women in Film', in A. Moran and T. O'Regan (eds), *An Australian Film Reader*, Sydney, Currency Press, 1985, p. 308.
3. R. Horrocks, 'Alternatives: Experimental Film Making in New Zealand', in J. Dennis and J. Bieringa (eds), *Film in Aotearoa New Zealand*, Wellington, Victoria University Press, 1992, p. 71.
4. See P. Adams Sitney, *Visionary Film: The American Avant-Garde 1943–1978*, New York, Oxford University Press, 1974. Note that Sitney uses the term 'psychodrama' in a different context to Horrocks (whose work was cited in Chapter 3). In Sitney's discussion of the 'trance film' of the US avant-garde beginning with Maya Deren, he links the psychodrama element with the dream and the surrealist tradition of 'a drama of psychological revelation', wherein 'the protagonist is the passive victim of the action of the film' (p. 100). This is certainly relevant, in terms of the influence of the American avant-garde on short film-makers coming out of the experimental traditions.
5. For more details, see S. Lawson, 'Serious Undertakings', in Moran and O'Regan (eds), *An Australian Film Reader*.
6. Ibid., p. 331.
7. *Shadow Panic* won awards at the American Film and Video Festival (1990) and the Australian Film Institute; Sally Bongers was nominated for Best Cinematography in the non-features section.
8. Film review publicity available from Cinenova Women's Distribution, London.
9. Maya Deren's poetic shorts *Meshes of the Afternoon* (1943), *At Land* (1944) and *Ritual in Transfigured Time* (1946) all link the unconscious with female identity.
10. A. Martin, 'The Short Film', in S. Murray (ed.), *Australian Cinema*, NSW, Allen and Unwin AFC, 1994, p. 201.
11. Horrocks, 'Alternatives', p. 76.
12. For *A Girl's Own Story*, Bongers won an Australian Film Award for Best Cinematography in the non-features section and she was nominated again

in 1989 for *Sweetie*, the first 35mm Australian feature to have been shot by a woman.
13. J. Campion, 'A Girl's Own Story', *Alternative Cinema*, vol. 11, no. 4, 1983/84, p. 31.
14. 'The Lady Killers', *Mirabella*, February 1995, p. 88.
15. Horrocks, 'Alternatives', p. 77.
16. Ibid., p. 78.

5. Other Identities (pp. 46–59)
1. M. Mita, 'The Soul and the Image', in J. Dennis and J. Bieringa (eds), *Film in Aotearoa New Zealand*, Wellington, Victoria University Press, 1992, p. 52.
2. B. Barclay, 'Amongst Landscapes', in Dennis and Bieringa (eds), *Film in Aotearoa New Zealand*, p. 123.
3. Mita, 'The Soul and the Image', p. 51.
4. I. Bertrand and W. Routt, 'The Big Bad Combine: Some Aspects of National Aspirations and International Constraints in the Australian Cinema, 1896–1929', in A. Moran and T. O'Regan (eds), *The Australian Screen*, Victoria, Penguin Books Australia, 1989.
5. K. Jennings, *Sites of Difference: Cinematic Representations of Aboriginality and Gender*, Victoria, Australian Film Institute, 1993.
6. Ibid., p. 49.
7. J. O'Shea, 'A Charmed Life', in Dennis and Bieringa (eds), *Film in Aotearoa New Zealand*, p. 18.
8. Ibid., p. 19.
9. R. Campbell, 'Eight Documentaries', in Dennis and Bieringa (eds), *Film in Aotearoa New Zealand*.
10. Jennings, *Sites of Difference*, p. 61.
11. T. Moffat, quoted in publicity sheet from Govett-Brewster Art Gallery, Australia, 10 August 1994.
12. Jennings, *Sites of Difference*, p. 70.
13. B. Gosden, programme notes to accompany screening of *Mauri* in July 1988.
14. Ibid.

6. Child's-eye view (pp. 60–72)
1. D. Stratton, *The Avocado Plantation: Boom and Bust in the Australian Film Industry*, Sydney, MacMillan, 1990, p. 369.
2. L. Francke, 40th London Film Festival Programme (7–24 November 1996), p. 47.
3. S. Gristwood, 'Just Campion', *Midweek*, 28 October–1 November 1993, p. 14.

7. Celluloid Sisters (pp. 73–85)
1. Note that there are also good and bad sisters in *Mildred Pierce* (Michael Curtiz, 1945). Further details can be found in C. Gledhill (ed.), *Home is*

Where the Heart is: Studies in Melodrama and the Women's Film, London, BFI, 1987.
2. 'Gillian Armstrong Interviewed by Raffaele Caputo', *Cinema Papers 90*, October 1992, p. 6.
3. 'I try to capture a moment, a feeling the way still photographers do.' Jane Campion, quoted in G. Andrew, 'Mad Lands', *Time Out*, no. 1026, 18 April 1990, pp. 14–15.
4. 'The key thing I was working with was the inside–outside thing, the way you can see outside from both ways (from the front and the back of the house).' 'Gillian Armstrong Interviewed by Raffaele Caputo', p. 8.
5. 'Different Complexions: Jane Campion, an Interview', in J. Dennis and J. Bieringa (eds), *Film in Aotearoa New Zealand*, Wellington, Victoria University Press, 1992, p. 99.
6. C. Cannon, 'Gillian Armstrong's *The Last Days of Chez Nous*', unpublished MA project, 1995, p. 1.
7. L. Francke, 'The Last Days of Chez Nous', *Sight and Sound*, vol. 3, no. 3, March 1993, p. 43.
8. Raffaele Caputo, Review of *The Last Days of Chez Nous*, *Cinema Papers 90*, October 1992, p. 53.
9. 'Gillian Armstrong Interviewed by Raffaele Caputo', p. 8.

8. Disrupting the Family (pp. 86–96)
1. A. Maclean, 'Car Crush Views: Miro Bilbrough Talks with Alison Maclean about Her First Feature-length Film – *Crush*', *Illusions*, no. 21/22, Winter 1993, p. 8.
2. Ibid.
3. L. Francke, 'Dark Side', *Sight and Sound*, vol. 3, no. 4, April 1993, p. 18.
4. L. Francke, Review of *Dallas Doll*, *Sight and Sound*, vol. 5, no. 2, February 1995, pp. 43–4.

9. Women Displaced (pp. 97–108)
1. D. Stratton, *The Avocado Plantation: Boom and Bust in the Australian Film Industry*, Sydney, Macmillan, 1990, p. 368.
2. Ibid., pp. 366–7.
3. V. Glaessner, Review of *High Tide*, *Monthly Film Bulletin*, vol. 55, no. 659, December 1988, p. 364.
4. B. McFarlane and G. Mayer, *New Australian Cinema: Sources and Parallels in American and British Film*, Cambridge/New York/Oakleigh, Cambridge University Press, 1992, p. 86.
5. N. Norman, 'The Film That's Dividing London's Dinner Parties', *Evening Standard*, London, 7 February 1994.
6. S. Gristwood, 'Just Campion', *Midweek*, 28 October–1 November 1993.
7. L. Francke, Review of *The Piano*, *Sight and Sound*, vol. 3, no. 11, November 1993, pp. 50–1.
8. V. Hazel, 'Disjointed Articulations: The Politics of Voice and Jane Campion's *The Piano*', *Women's Studies Journal*, vol. 10, no. 2, September 1994.

9. D. Eggleton, 'Grimm Fairytale of the South Seas', *Illusions*, no. 23, Winter 1994, pp. 3–5.

10. The Wave Rolls On (pp. 109–26)
1. 'Film and Video Listing', C. Barton and D. Lawler-Dormer (eds), *Alter/Image: Feminism and Representation in New Zealand Art 1973–1993*, Wellington City Gallery and Auckland City Art Gallery, 1993, p. 101.
2. See C. J. Clover, *Men, Women and Chainsaws: Gender in the Modern Horror Film*, London, BFI, 1992.
3. Nash's documentary-drama *Speaking Out* (about young girls at risk) won an award at the Australian Video Festival in 1986 and her experimental drama *Shadow Panic* was awarded prizes by the Film and Video Festival in 1990 and the Australian Film Institute.
4. S. Hall, Review of *Love Serenade*, *Sydney Morning Herald*, 10 October 1996.
5. 'Think Global, Film Local', *SMH Metro*, 20–26 September 1996.
6. Ibid.
7. From Director's Notes, provided by the New Zealand Film Commission.
8. Ibid.

Select Bibliography

This list contains suggested further reading in key areas covered by the book. As well as the books and articles listed here, readers will find it useful to consult journals such as *Alternative Cinema*, *Cinema Papers*, *Film Quarterly*, *Illusions*, *Monthly Film Bulletin* and *Sight and Sound*, as well as periodicals specialising in feminism and/or popular culture.

1. New Zealand and Australian Cinema
Cairns, B. and Martin, H., *Shadows on the Wall: A Study of Seven New Zealand Feature Films*, Auckland, Longman Paul, 1994.
Dennis, J. and Bieringa, J. (eds), *Film in Aotearoa New Zealand*, Wellington, Victoria University Press, 1992.
Dermody, S. and Jacka, E. (eds), *The Imaginary Industry: Australian Film in the Late 80s*, North Ryde NSW, AFTRS, 1988.
McFarlane, B. and Mayer, G., *New Australian Cinema: Sources and Parallels in American and British Film*, Cambridge/New York/Oakleigh, Cambridge University Press, 1992.
Moran, A. and O'Regan, T. (eds), *An Australian Film Reader*, Sydney, Currency Press, 1985.
—— (eds), *The Australian Screen*, Victoria, Penguin Books Australia, 1989.
Murray, S. (ed.), *Back of Beyond, Discovering Australian Film and TV*, Sydney, Australian Film Commission, 1988.
—— (ed.), *Australian Cinema*, NSW, Allen and Unwin/AFC, 1994.
Rattigan, N., *Images of Australia: 100 Films of the New Australian Cinema*, Dallas, Southern Methodist University Press, 1991.
Reid, N., *A Decade of New Zealand Film: 'Sleeping Dogs' to 'Came a Hot Friday'*, Dunedin, John McIndoe, 1986.
Stratton, D., *The Avocado Plantation: Boom and Bust in the Australian Film Industry*, Sydney, Macmillan, 1990.
Turner, G. (ed.), *Nation, Culture, Text*, London, Routledge, 1993.

2. Feminist Approaches to Cinema
Alysen, B., 'Australian Women in Film', in A. Moran and T. O'Regan (eds), *An Australian Film Reader*, Sydney, Currency Press, 1985.

Benjamin, J. and Maclean, A., 'Revolving Clotheslines and Morris Minors: A Discussion of New Zealand Film-making with Gaylene Preston', *Alternative Cinema*, vol. 11, no. 4, Summer 1983–84.

Blonski, A. Creed, B., and Freiberg, F. (eds), *Don't Shoot Darling! Women's Independent Film-making in Australia*, Richmond Victoria, Greenhouse, 1987.

Clover, C. J., *Men, Women and Chainsaws: Gender in the Modern Horror Film*, London, BFI, 1992.

Creed, B., *The Monstrous-Feminine: Women in the Horror Film*, London, Routledge, 1993.

Davis, S., Maclean, A., and Todd, H., 'She Through He: Images of Women in New Zealand Feature Films', *Alternative Cinema*, vol. 11, no. 4, Summer 1983–84.

Doane, M. A. *Femmes Fatales: Feminism, Film Theory, Psychoanalysis*, New York/London, Routledge, 1991.

Gledhill, C. (ed.), *Home is Where the Heart is: Studies in Melodrama and the Women's Film*, London, BFI, 1987.

Hardy, A., 'Tales of Ordinary Goodness – Feminism in New Zealand Film', *Illusions*, no. 12, 1989, pp. 14–21.

—— 'Sweetie: A Song in the Desert', *Illusions*, no. 15, 1990.

Hazel, V., 'Disjointed Articulations: The Politics of Voice and Jane Campion's The Piano', *Women's Studies Journal*, vol. 10, no. 2, September 1994.

Kaplan, E. Ann (ed.), *Women in Film Noir*, London, BFI, 1978.

Mulvey, L., 'Visual Pleasure and Narrative Cinema', *Screen*, vol. 16, no. 3, Autumn 1975.

Stern, L., 'Independent Feminist Film-making in Australia', in A. Moran and T. O'Regan (eds), *An Australian Film Reader*, Sydney, Currency Press, 1985.

Watson, R., 'Naughty Girls' Films', *Illusions*, no. 15, 1990.

3. Experimental and Lesbian Cinema

Adams Sitney, P., *Visionary Film: The American Avant-Garde 1943–1978*, New York, Oxford University Press, 1974.

Gever, M., Greyson, J., and Parmar, P. (eds), *Queer Looks: Perspectives on Lesbian and Gay Film and Video*, London/New York, Routledge, 1993.

Mellencamp, P., *Indiscretions: Avant-Garde Film, Video and Feminism*, Bloomington/Indianapolis, Indiana University Press, 1990.

Rabinovitz, L., *Points of Resistance: Women, Power and Politics in the New York Avant-Garde Cinema 1943–1971*, Urbana/Chicago, University of Illinois Press, 1991.

Thoms, A., *Polemics for a New Cinema*, Sydney, Wild and Woolley, 1978.

Weiss, A., *Vampires and Violets: Lesbians in the Cinema*, London, Jonathan Cape, 1992.

Wilton, T. (ed.), *Immortal, Invisible: Lesbians and the Moving Image*, London, Routledge, 1995.

4. Indigenous Cinema

Barclay, B., *Our Own Image*, Auckland, Longman Paul, 1990.

—— 'Amongst Landscapes', in J. Dennis and J. Bieringa (eds), *Film in Aotearoa New Zealand*, Wellington, Victoria University Press, 1992.

Blythe, M., *Naming the Other: Images of Maori in NZ Film and Television*, Metuchen, New Jersey Scarecrow Press, London, 1994.

Edwards, S., 'Cinematic Imperialism and Maori Cultural Identity', *Illusions*, no. 10, March 1989.

Hickling-Hudson, A., 'White Construction of Black Identity in Australian Films About Aborigines', *Literature and Film Quarterly*, vol. 18, no. 4, 1990.

Hollinsworth, D., 'Discourses on Aboriginality and the Politics of Identity in Urban Australia', *Oceania*, vol. 63, no. 2, 1992.

Jennings, K., *Sites of Difference: Cinematic Representations of Aboriginality and Gender*, Victoria, Australian Film Insititute, 1993.

Langton, M., *'Well I Heard it on the Radio and I Saw it on the Television...'*, Sydney, Australian Film Commission, 1993.

Mita, M., 'The Soul and the Image', in J. Dennis and J. Bieringa (eds), *Film in Aotearoa New Zealand*, Wellington, Victoria University Press, 1992.

Moore, C. and Muecke, S., 'Racism and the Representation of Aborigines in Films', *Australian Journal of Cultural Studies*, vol. 2, no. 1, 1984.

Filmography

All This and Heaven Too, USA, 1940, Anatole Litvak
Anatomy of a Friendship, New Zealand, 1973, Alexis Hunter (20 mins)
Angel at My Table, An, New Zealand, 1990, Jane Campion
Beach, The, New Zealand, 1996, Dorthe Scheffmann (8 mins)
Bedevil, Australia, 1993, Tracey Moffat
Black Veil, Australia, 1987, Monica Pellizzari (13 mins)
Broken Barrier, New Zealand, 1952, John O'Shea/Roger Mirams
Came a Hot Friday, New Zealand, 1985, Ian Mune
Cars That Ate Paris, The, Australia, 1974, Peter Weir
Celia, Australia, 1988, Ann Turner
Chant of Jimmie Blacksmith, The, Australia, 1978, Fred Schepisi
Cheaters, The, Australia, 1930, Phyllis, Paulette and Isobel McDonagh
Crocodile Dundee, Australia, 1986, Peter Faiman
Crush, New Zealand, 1992, Alison Maclean
Dallas Doll, Australia, 1994, Ann Turner
Dark Mirror, The, USA, 1946, Robert Siodmak
Eliza Fraser, Australia, 1976, Tim Burstall
Fatal Attraction, USA, 1987, Adrian Lyne
Fires Within, USA, 1991, Gillian Armstrong
Fistful of Flies, Australia, 1996, Monica Pellizzari
Fringe Dwellers, The, Australia, 1986, Bruce Beresford
Floating Life, Australia, 1996, Clara Law
Gallipoli, Australia, 1981, Peter Weir
Getting of Wisdom, The, Australia, 1977, Bruce Beresford
Girl's Own Story, A, Australia, 1984, Jane Campion (26 mins)
Goodbye Pork Pie, New Zealand, 1981, Geoff Murphy
Hand That Rocks the Cradle, The, USA, 1992, Curtis Hanson
Heathers, USA, 1989, Michael Lehmann
High Tide, Australia, 1987, Gillian Armstrong
Hinemoa, New Zealand, 1914, George Tarr
Hooks and Feelers, New Zealand, 1982, Melanie Read (50 mins)
I Want to be Joan, New Zealand, 1977, Stephanie Beth (doc)
Innocents, The, GB, 1961, Jack Clayton

Irene 59, New Zealand, 1981, Shereen Maloney (12 mins)
I've Heard the Mermaids Singing, Canada, 1987, Patricia Rozema
Jeddah, Australia, 1955, Charles Chauval
Jezebel, USA, 1938, William Wyler
Just Desserts, Australia, 1993, Monica Pellizzari (12 mins)
King Pin, New Zealand, 1985, Mike Walker
Kitchen Sink, New Zealand, 1989, Alison Maclean (14 mins)
Landslides, Australia, 1986, Sarah Gibson and Susan Lambert (75 mins)
Last Days of Chez Nous, The, Australia, 1990, Gillian Armstrong
Letter from an Unknown Woman, USA, 1948, Max Ophuls
Life in the Kitchen, New Zealand, 1988, Sally Smith (7 mins)
Love Serenade, Australia, 1996, Shirley Barrett
Mad Max, Australia, 1979, George Miller
Mauri, New Zealand, 1988, Merata Mita
Mermaids, USA, 1990, Richard Benjamin
Mokopuna, New Zealand, 1992, Whetu Fala (6 mins)
Mr Wrong, New Zealand, 1985, Gaylene Preston
Mrs Soffel, USA, 1984, Gillian Armstrong
My American Cousin, Canada, 1985, Sandy Wilson
My Brilliant Career, Australia, 1979, Gillian Armstrong
My Survival as an Aboriginal, Australia, 1979, Essie Coffey (doc)
Ngati, New Zealand, 1987, Barry Barclay
Nice Coloured Girls, Australia, 1987, Tracey Moffat (18 mins)
Night Cries, Australia, 1989, Tracey Moffat (17 mins)
Not Just a Pretty Face, Australia, 1983, Gillian Armstrong (doc)
Now and Then, USA, 1995, Leslie Linka Glatter
O Tamaiti, New Zealand, 1996, Sima Urale (15 mins)
On Guard, Australia, 1983, Susan Lambert (51 mins)
Only the Brave, Australia, 1994, Ana Kokkinos
Other Halves, New Zealand, 1984, John Laing
Patu!, New Zealand, 1983, Merata Mita (doc)
Peel, Australia, 1983, Jane Campion (9 mins)
Piano, The, Australia/New Zealand/France, 1993, Jane Campion
Picnic at Hanging Rock, Australia, 1975, Peter Weir
Pictures, New Zealand, 1981, Michael Black
Psycho, USA, 1960, Alfred Hitchcock
Rabbit on the Moon, Australia, 1988, Monica Pellizzari (13 mins)
Razorback, Australia, 1984, Russell Mulcahy
Repulsion, GB, 1965, Roman Polanski
Rewi's Last Stand, New Zealand, 1925 and 1940, Rudall Hayward
Romance of Hinemoa, The, GB, 1926, Gustav Pauli
Romantic New Zealand, New Zealand, 1934 (government doc)
Serendipity, Australia, 1992, Karen Borger (17 mins)
Serious Undertakings, Australia, 1983, Helen Grace and Erika Addis (28 mins)
Shadow Panic, Australia, 1989, Margot Nash (25 mins)
Single White Female, USA, 1992, Barbet Schroeder
Some of My Best Friends are Women, New Zealand, 1975, Deirdre MacCartin (30 mins)

Song of Air, A, Australia, 1987, Merilee Bennett (23 mins)
Speaking Out, Australia, 1986, Margot Nash (doc)
Stolen Life, USA, 1946, Curtis Bernhardt
Storm Boy, Australia, 1977, Henri Safran
Stroke, New Zealand, 1993, Christine Jeffs (8 mins)
Sweetie, Australia, 1989, Jane Campion
Swimming, Australia, 1990, Belinda Chayko (11 mins)
Tangata Whenua, New Zealand, 1974, Barry Barclay and Michael King (doc)
Terra Nullius, Australia, 1992, Anne Pratten (21 mins)
This is New Zealand, New Zealand, 1971, Hugh McDonald (doc)
Threshold, New Zealand, 1971, Richard Phelps (18 mins)
Time Trap, New Zealand, 1991, Sally Smith (17 mins)
To Love a Maori, New Zealand, 1972, Rudall Hayward
Trial Run, New Zealand, 1984, Melanie Read
Two Minutes Silence, Australia, 1934, Phyllis, Paulette and Isobel McDonagh
Utu, New Zealand, 1983, Geoff Murphy
Vacant Possession, Australia, 1995, Margot Nash
Vigil, New Zealand, 1984, Vincent Ward
Walkabout, Australia, 1971, Nicolas Roeg
Whistle Down the Wind, GB, 1961, Bryan Forbes
Wuthering Heights, USA, 1940, William Wyler
Yeah, Mostafa! Australia, 1993, Ali Higson (11 mins)

Other Recommended Titles
Amelia Rose Towers, Australia, 1992, Jackie Farkas (10 mins)
Annie's Coming Out, Australia, 1984, Gil Brealey
Bread and Roses, New Zealand, 1993, Gaylene Preston
Broken Skin, New Zealand, 1990, Anna Campion (11 mins)
Damning, Australia, 1992, Penny Fowler-Smith (11 mins)
Father is Nothing, The, Australia, 1991, Leone Knight (10 mins)
Flowers by Request, Australia, 1992, Susan Wallace (18 mins)
Hinekaro Goes on a Picnic and Blows Up Another Obelisk, New Zealand, 1995, Christine Parker (14 mins)
In Loving Memory, Australia, 1992, Leone Knight (5 mins)
Invisible Hand, The, New Zealand, 1992, Athina Tsoulis (11 mins)
Jumping the Gun, Australia, 1993, Jane Schneider (10 mins)
La Vie en Rose, New Zealand, 1994, Ana Reeves (7 mins)
Life on Earth as I Know It, Australia, 1989, Penny McDonald (8 mins)
Mini-skirted Dynamo, The, Australia, 1996, Rivka Hartman (55 mins)
Mon Desir, New Zealand, 1991, Nicky Marshall (15 mins)
Mr Reliable, Australia, 1995, Nadia Tass
Night Work, Australia, 1994, Jane Schneider (12 mins)
Peach, New Zealand, 1993, Christine Parker (16 mins)
Proof, Australia, 1991, Jocelyn Moorhouse
Punch Me in the Stomach, New Zealand/Canada, 1996, Francine Zuckerman (72 mins)
Rational Life, The, Australia, 1989, Debbie Lee (10 mins)

Ruby and Rata, New Zealand, 1990, Gaylene Preston
Send a Gorilla, New Zealand, 1988, Melanie Read
Silent One, The, New Zealand, 1984, Yvonne MacKay
Silver City, Australia, 1984, Sophia Turkiewicz
Sinistre, New Zealand, 1989, Nikola Caro (10 mins)
Song of Ceylon, Australia, 1985, Laleen Jayamanne (51 mins)
Taunt, New Zealand, 1982, Alison Maclean (17 mins)
This Marching Girl Thing, Australia, 1994, Kelli Simpson (19 mins)
Two Friends, Australia, 1986, Jane Campion (75 mins)
Waiting, Australia, 1990, Jackie McKimmie
War Stories Our Mother Never Told Us, New Zealand, 1995, Gaylene Preston (doc)
You Require Filmic Pleasure, New Zealand, 1987, Marilyn Tweedie (variable length)

In the UK, many of the above titles are distributed by Cinenova, 113 Roman Road, Bethnal Green, London E2 0QN; Tel: 0181 981 6828.

Index

Aboriginal people
  cinematic representations of 48–9
  role in making documentaries 50
  role in making feature films 51
Aboriginal women's films 51
  Nice Coloured Girls 51–4, 52
  Night Cries 54–5
  Terra Nullius 55
An Angel at My Table 68–70, 69
Armstrong, Gillian
  High Tide 97, 98–102, 103
  Last Days of Chez Nous 74, 75, 80–5
  return to Australia 74, 97
  and 'women's pictures' 12
  see also My Brilliant Career
art-film influences in High Tide 101
Australia
  1970s revival of film industry 9, 11
  contemporary context of film-making 6
  cultural context of film-making 4, 5–6
  funding of film industry 1–2, 3
  women's films 3, 32
  landscape theme 6, 9
  links with New Zealand film industry 7, 102
  national culture and identity 4, 5–6
  in My Brilliant Career 16
  in Serious Undertakings 34, 36
  perceptions of USA in Dallas Doll 93–4
  women's cinematic traditions 117–20
  compared with New Zealand 7–8, 113–14
  emergence and nature of 6–7, 8, 12, 32
  women's involvement in film industry 3
  see also Aboriginal people; Aboriginal women's films
Australian Film Commission (AFC) 2, 3
Avant Garde Film Making Group (Melbourne) 32

Barclay, Barry 47, 50, 51
Barrett, Shirley, Love Serenade 123
Batten, Juliet 5
Beach, The 125
Bennett, Merilee, A Song of Air 37–40, 39
Bongers, Sally 36, 41–2
Broken Barrier 48

Campion, Jane
  An Angel at My Table 68–70, 69
  background 41
  feminist influences 44–5
  Girl's Own Story, A 41–2, 43, 76

return to New Zealand 73–4, 97
Sweetie 41–2, 73, 74–5, 76–80, 79, 81
The Piano 97–8, 102–8, *106*
Canada
  funding of film industry 3–4
  women's involvement in film industry 3–4
Celia 62–5, *63*
  compared with *Dallas Doll* 92–3
Chayko, Belinda, *Swimming* 40–1
children
  in British cinema 60–1
  Hollywood representations of 60, 72
  perspectives in women's films of 60, 61–2, 71–2
  An Angel at My Table 68–70, *69*
  Celia 62–5, *63*
  Rabbit on the Moon 65–8, *67*
  Serendipity 71
  see also family issues in women's films
Coffey, Essie 50
colonisation
  images in *The Piano* 107–8
  issues in *Vacant Possession* 121
Creative Film and Video Fund (later Creative New Zealand) 2
Crush 86–92, *88*
  cultural intrusions 89–90
  as example of psychodrama 114
  family 89, 91–2
  identities and roles 87–9
  landscape 90–1
  melodrama, horror and *film noir* influences 91–2
  relationship with *Kitchen Sink* 86
cultural difference, in *Just Desserts* and *Yeah, Mostafa!* 112
culture
  context of Australasian film-making 4–6
  depictions of cultural intrusions 89–90, 93–4
  and representations of women in short films

Just Desserts 112–13
Mokopuna 110–11
Yeah, Mostafa! 111–12
see also ethnicity; indigenous women's films

Dallas Doll 92–6
  characterisation of USA 93–4
  compared with *Celia* 92–3
  humorous and political nature of 95–6
  representations of middle class suburbia 94–5
  role plays 93
  stars of 92
Deren, Maya 37
displaced women
  in *High Tide* and *The Piano* 97
  influence of Law's background on *Floating Life* 123
  influence of Urale's background on *O Tamaiti* 124
documentaries
  made by indigenous people 50–1
  made by women 31, 32–3

ethnicity
  as feature of women's films 7, 46
  see also culture; indigenous women's films; race
ethnographic films, of Maori people 47

Fala, Wheta, *Mokopuna* 110–11
family issues in women's films 6–7, 29
  disruption by female protagonist in *Crush* 89, 91–2
  Floating Life 123
  Girl's Own Story, A 42
  High Tide 98–102, *103*
  Only the Brave 117–20
  Song of Air 37–40
  Swimming 40–1
  Trial Run 19, 23–5, 29
  Vacant Possession 121, 122
  see also children; sisters

female predators
    in *Crush* 86–92, *88*
    in *Dallas Doll* 92–6
feminist influences in women's films 32, 33
    My Brilliant Career 10
    Serious Undertakings 34–6, *35*
    Shadow Panic 36–7
    Time Trap 115
    Trial Run 27
feminist psychodrama, New Zealand tradition of 8, 28–9, 33, 114–17
    Crush 114
    Girl's Own Story, A 41–2, *43*
    Kitchen Sink 41, 44
    Stroke 116–17
    Sweetie 73
    Time Trap 114–16
    Trial Run 28, 114
feminist theories of silence and oppression 104–5
Film Finance Corporation 2
film noir influences in *Crush* 91–2
Floating Life 123–4
Frame, Janet 68
Fringe Dwellers, The 49
funding of film industry
    in Australia 1–2, 3, 32
    in New Zealand 1–3, 32

gender debates 109–10
gender roles and cultural issues in women's short films 110
    Just Desserts 112–13
    Mokopuna 110–11
    Yeah, Mostafa! 111–12
Getting of Wisdom, The 9
Girl's Own Story, A 41–2, *43*
    link with *Sweetie* 41–2, 76
Grace, Helen, *Serious Undertakings* 34–6, *35*

Hazel, Valerie 105
High Tide 98–102, *103*
    female input 98
    landscape 97, 100–1
    marginal existences 100–1
    melodrama and art-film influences 101
    performance and masquerade 97, 98–100
Higson, Ali, *Yeah, Mostafa!* 111–12
Hinemoa 48
Hollywood
    representations of children 60, 72
    representations of sisters 73
    women's involvement in film industry 4
horror, in *Crush* 92
Hunter, Alexis 32

Ikin, Bridget 86
immigration *see* displaced women
indigenous people *see* Aboriginal people; Maori people
indigenous women's films 46, 59
    context of 46–50
    Mauri 55–9
    Nice Coloured Girls 51–4, *52*
    Night Cries 54–5
    Terra Nullius 55

Jane Eyre, parallels with *My Brilliant Career* 10–11
Jeddah 48–9
Jeff, Christine, *Stroke* 116–17
Jennings, Karen 48–9, 50
Jupp, James 5–6
Just Desserts 112–13

Kitchen Sink 41, 44
    relationship with *Crush* 86
Kokkinos, Ana, *Only the Brave* 117–20, *119*

Lambert, Susan 32
land
    images of colonisation in *The Piano* 107–8
    and place in *Floating Life* 123
    rights and ecology in *Vacant Possession* 121, 122

landscape
  Australian preoccupation with 6, 9
  as feature of women's films 7, 29, 37
  Crush 90–1
  Floating Life 124
  High Tide 97, 100–1
  The Piano 97
  Trial Run 19, 20, 21, 22–3
  New Zealand preoccupation with 6, 19–20
  versus melodrama in *My Brilliant Career* 12–13
language, politics of voice in *The Piano* 104–5
Last Days of Chez Nous 80–5
  background 74
  compared with *Sweetie* 74–5, 80–1
Law, Clara
  background 123
  Floating Life 123–4
lesbian representations in psychodrama 114–15
Life in the Kitchen 115
Love Serenade 123

McDonald, James 47
Maclean, Alison
  background 41
  Crush 86–92, 88, 114
  Kitchen Sink 41, 44–5
Maori people
  cinematic representations of 47–8, 49
  family theme in *Crush* 89
  heritage in *Mokopuna* 110–11
  and images of colonisation in *The Piano* 107, 108
  role in making documentaries 50–1
  role in making feature films 51
Maori women's films, *Mauri* 55–9
Martin, Adrian 41
masquerade and performance
  in *High Tide* 97, 98–100
  in *The Piano* 97–8, 105–7

Mauri 55–9
Méliès, Gaston 48
melodrama
  in *Crush* 91
  in *High Tide* 101
  in *My Brilliant Career* 12, 13
Mita, Merata 47
  Mauri 55–9
  Patu! 50–1
Moffat, Tracy 51
  Nice Coloured Girls 51–4, 52
  Night Cries 54–5
Mokopuna 110–11
Mr Wrong 28
My Brilliant Career 9–10, 15, 17–18
  cinematic influences 11–12
  feminist nature of 10
  opposition between nature and culture 12–16
  opposition between wild and tame 16–17
  parallels with *Jane Eyre* 10–11
  stars of 12
My Survival as an Aboriginal 50

Nash, Margot
  career 120–1
  Shadow Panic 36–7, 45
  Vacant Possession 29, 120, 121–2
national culture and identity
  of Australia 4, 5–6
  in *My Brilliant Career* 16
  in *Serious Undertakings* 34, 36
  of New Zealand 5
New Australian Cinema 9, 11
New Zealand
  Campion's return to 73–4, 97
  contemporary context of film-making 6
  cultural context of film-making 5, 6
  cultural intrusion of America in *Crush* 89–90
  family in women's films 29
  funding of film industry 1–3
  women's films 2–3, 32

landscape theme 6, 19–20, 29
links with Australian film
    industry 7, 102
national identity 5
women's cinematic tradition
    compared with Australia 7–8,
      113–14
    emergence and nature of 6–7,
      8, 32–3
    see also feminist psychodrama
women's involvement in film
    industry 2–3
    see also Maori people
New Zealand Film Commission
    (NZFC) 2, 3
Nice Coloured Girls 51–4, 52
Night Cries 54–5

O Tamaiti 124
Only the Brave 117–20, 119

Patu! 50–1
Pauli, Gustav 48
Pellizzari, Monica
    career 68
    Just Desserts 112–13
    Rabbit on the Moon 65–8, 67
performance see masquerade and
    performance
Piano, The 102–8, 106
    cross-cultural input 102
    images of colonisation 107–8
    landscape 97
    masquerade 97–8, 105–7
    politics of voice 104–5
    reactions to 102
Picnic at Hanging Rock 9
Pratten, Anne 55
Preston, Gaylene 28, 32
Psycho 25
psychodrama see feminist
    psychodrama
psychological thrillers, reworking
    of 25–8

Rabbit on the Moon 65–8, 67

race
    and gender roles represented in
      women's short films 110
    Just Desserts 112–13
    Mokopuna 110–11
    Yeah, Mostafa! 111–12
    see also Aboriginal people;
      culture; ethnicity; Maori
      people
Rattigan, Neil 4, 10
Read, Melanie
    career 20
    involvement in Time Trap 115
    see also Trial Run
Rewi's Last Stand 48
'rites-of-passage' films 9, 61, 62,
    72, 112–13
Romance of Hinemoa, The 48

Scheffmann, Dorthe, The Beach 125
Serendipity 71
Serious Undertakings 34–6, 35
sexuality
    debates 109–10
    sexualised female friendships in
      psychodrama 114–15
Shadow Panic 36–7, 45
Short Film Fund 2
short films
    background of 30–3
    children's perceptions in
      Rabbit on the Moon 65–8, 67
      Serendipity 71
    culture and gender roles in 110
      Just Desserts 112–13
      Mokopuna 110–11
      Yeah, Mostafa! 111–12
    female identity in families
      Song of Air 37–40, 39
      Swimming 40–1
    feminist influences 32, 33
      Serious Undertakings 34–6, 35
      Shadow Panic 36–7
    importance of 30
    indigenous women's
      Nice Coloured Girls 51–4, 52
      Night Cries 54–5
      Terra Nullius 55

psychodramas
    A Girl's Own Story 41–2, 43
    Kitchen Sink 44
    as route into film industry 7, 30–1
silence, politics of voice in *The Piano* 104–5
sisters
    in Hollywood films 73
    in *Last Days of Chez Nous* 80–5
    in *Last Days of Chez Nous* compared with *Sweetie* 74–5, 80–1
    in *Love Serenade* 123
    in *Sweetie* 76–80, 79
Smith, Sally
    Life in the Kitchen 115
    Time Trap 114–16
Song of Air 37–40, 39
Stroke 116–17
suburbia, in *Dallas Doll* 94–5
Sweetie 76–80, 79
    compared with *Last Days of Chez Nous* 74–5, 80–1
    link with *A Girl's Own Story* 41–2, 76
    New Zealand background to 73
Swimming 40–1
Sydney Film Makers Co-op 32

Tangata Whenua 50
tax concessions, for film-making 1–2
Terra Nullius 55
Time Trap 114–16
To Love a Maori 49
Trial Run 26
    as example of Psychodrama 28, 114
    family theme 19, 23–5, 29
    female input 20
    as feminist film 19, 27
    genre influences 19
    landscape theme 19, 20, 21, 22–3
    local cinematic context 19–20
    opposition between natural and unnatural 22–3
    as reworking of psychological thriller 25–8
    run as central motif 21–2
Turner, Ann
    Celia 62–5, 63
    Dallas Doll 92–6

Urale, Sima, *O Tamaiti* 124
USA
    cultural intrusion of 89–90, 93–4
    see also Hollywood

Vacant Possession 29, 120, 121–2
victims, in psychological thrillers 25, 27

women
    in Australian film industry 3
    in Canadian film industry 3–4
    in Hollywood film industry 4
    in New Zealand film industry 2–3
    short films as route into film industry for 7, 30–1
    see also displaced women; gender roles
Women's Film Fund (WFF) 3

Yeah, Mostafa! 111–12

Index by Judith Lavender

Also available from Scarlet Press

Women and Film
A Sight and Sound Reader
Edited by Pam Cook and Philip Dodd

Covering cinema from its earliest days to the present, this anthology is a major contribution to a feminist understanding of film. With more than 30 essays by distinguished critics and historians, this provocative and rich collection moves from Lillian Gish and women and animation through studies of stars such as Audrey Hepburn and Hattie McDaniel to arguments around the Alien trilogy and the work of important contemporary directors such as Jane Campion, Sally Potter and Mira Nair.

'Consistently surprising and accessible, this is contemporary criticism at its best – as smart as Clarice Starling, as gutsy as Thelma and Louise and as agile as Ripley.' Suzanne Moore, journalist and film critic

'*Women and Film*'s scope and depth, its variety – from cultural criticism to one-to-one interview – reflect an important new direction in the changing attitudes and debates that surround the representation of women in all aspects of contemporary cinema.' Susan Seidelman, director

40 illustrations
ISBN Paperback 1 85727 081 9